EX U OUT

HOW I FIRED THE SHAME COMMITTEE

JOHN J. SMID

Acknowledgements

I would like to thank the following people for helping to make this journey and book possible:

God, our Creator, for His unending grace and intimate love for me

My wife, Vileen, for her patience and grace to walk alongside me

Lisa Darden for challenging me to open my heart and mind to think differently

Michael Watt, my good friend, who has been beside me and supported me for many years

James Salazar, who has listened to all of my honest ramblings and responded with compassion

Kevin Diaz, for creative input and endless hours of editing and insightful wisdom

Joe Thweat, for spending hours reviewing this manuscript for me

Kevyn Bashore, for inspiration for this book from his photographic talent

EX'D OUT

For many encouraging friends who wish to remain anonymous

All of those who have told me over and over that I should write a book - because of you I have done it!

Dedication

I'd like to dedicate this book to the countless men and women who have wrestled with homosexuality and their understanding of God. I hope you will find God's loving embrace in such a way that you know without a doubt that you are loved. It is my hope that somewhere within these writings you will find peace.

Preface

By Jeremy Marks, Executive Director Courage - UK

The Christian faith is clearly a path fraught with dangers for disciples of Jesus Christ, because we place our hope in a God who is unseen. Evangelical Christians believe we are called to be Christ's messengers appointed to preach the Good News of the Kingdom of God and the forgiveness of sins. We are also called, every one of us, to repentance and a life of obedience to the Lordship of Christ, who paid the price for our sins, so that we might be forgiven. Repentance means wholeheartedly turning away from the ways of the world, the flesh and the devil. And most evangelical Christians down the generations have been convinced (until quite recently) that homosexuality is a work of the devil, spawned to make a travesty of the beauty of God's (heterosexual) creation. Indeed gay people have provided a convenient scapegoat for all of society's ills in recent generations. However, God has heard the cry of gay people and the Holy Spirit, who is still leading us into all truth, is today calling us to repent of our ignorance and prejudice towards gay people.

We live in a world where we see and hear plenty of popular preachers, all ready to tell us what God has to say to us (in exchange for a salary). They have left us in no doubt as to what they believe about homosexuality: most have believed it is sufficient to quote certain verses and condemn gay people, even though they know nothing about the subject at all. We have the Bible, the Word of God, which reveals God to mankind, whilst being capable of a variety of interpretations on every subject, including homosexuality. Each different interpretation has its enthusiastic exponents, whether that be on sexuality, end-times theology and everything in-between. Jesus promised to send us His Holy Spirit to lead us into all truth, which he must have promised to offer reassurance to his disciples at the time of his impending crucifixion. Yet the first Christian church was soon riven by disputes and differing views on what the Christian life and doctrine should look like. It was not long before the early Church made what must surely be its most catastrophic mistake by starting out on the basis of accepting people into the church if they held to the right doctrine as they perceived it, instead of heeding Jesus' observation that, "by their fruit you shall know them" (Matthew 7).

Little has changed in 2000 years since. Who are we to believe in today? We all seem to have to learn the hard way, too often trusting in popular charismatic leaders who seem confident they have the truth to share. But in the end, as John Smid's account proclaims here, it is only by coming to know Christ for ourselves that we discover the life-giving relationship with God that bears lasting good fruit and true freedom - to become the quietly confident and authentic person God made us to be.

John Smid's amazing story reveals his authenticity as a true follower of Christ. But the price of his freedom in Christ today meant first taking a long and tortuous journey encountering many seriously deep pitfalls along the way. Lacking confidence in himself at the outset, he believed and placed his hope in the teaching of apparently good but (as his story reveals) seriously misguided Christian people. The John Smid I have known for the past 25 years has revealed an all-too-rarely seen depth of humility, as he has carried out a merciless moral inventory of his own life and teaching in recent years, and publicly repented of all his mistakes and false teachings as he has come to realize them. Maybe John needed to, as his gay Christian critics have already pointed out, whilst his opponents from the conservative churches have already branded him a deceiver and a heretic. However, according to my observation through my life of 60 years now, I have never seen any Christian teacher anywhere who has been willing to make such an open and profound repentance from the heart.

What can we learn from John Smid's story? The simple yet glaringly prophetic contemporary message here is that it simply is not enough for Christian teachers to be good or well-meaning. Unless they introduce people to a personal life with Christ, they lead people up blind alleys. Too many prefer to preach a cheap gospel (which is no gospel at all) encouraging people to live a life working hard to improve one's self, according to their own understanding - so often taught as legal principles. As he reveals how they have nullified the life-giving Word of God, John has exposed them for what they are: blind leaders of the blind, as Jesus put it. But their message seems attractive because they offer hope and acceptance within their communities, for all who abide by their rules. Why does anyone do this? Because a life of personal self-discipline can seem an appealing substitute for a life lived in the grace and provision of God. It is something we can achieve without God by our own efforts, but the fruit is arrogance and pride, not the humility of Christ.

Jesus promised something different – that in this life we would have trouble (John 16:33). His lifestyle of loving service to others in which he restored dignity to every outcast, led to his crucifixion at the hands of his own people - who "hated him without cause". This is a path that many gay Christian people have had to walk.

John Smid's story will bring enormous hope and comfort to thousands of men and women who have struggled to tune their lives to the ex-gay message, only to end up disillusioned and profoundly disappointed. At the same time, he brings chastisement to all those teachers and ministry leaders who refuse to listen. Preferring to tow the party line, they do not even hunger to grow in Christ for themselves. None of them will want to read John's story except perhaps to pick holes in it. Thanks be to God, this book is a story of one man's immense courage as he has pursued his personal search for truth and authenticity as a gay Christian man. The John Smid I have been privileged to know these past 25 years is an example of a man who has truly come to know Jesus Christ as Lord.

Introduction

After twenty-three years of faithful service to hundreds, if not thousands of men and women through a formal ministry called Love In Action, I resigned in May of 2008.

I had been known worldwide as one of the stable men who fought fearlessly for the truth of God that He condemned the practice of homosexuality. The ministry I was involved in was one of the largest ministries which also included a residential program and was unparalleled by other models of ministry that proclaimed "Freedom from Homosexuality through Jesus Christ."

My work included public speaking and leading conferences on three continents and traveling throughout the United States, handing out thousands of pages of personally written material to people who were hurting. They were desiring to hear that God could and would dramatically change someone's sexuality so that homosexuality would no longer be a burden.

It was at the time of my resignation after several years of painful stress and personal challenges, that I chose not to make any plans for the future and prayed, "God, I don't want to contrive my future plans, so surprise me!"

During the next four years, I began to evaluate my previous years of ministry and realized that there was something new coming directly from God that was beginning to change my entire baseline of thought about Him, and about homosexuality. I also realized that I had made many mistakes. So, I began to take a deep personal inventory and chose to write an extensive weekly web-blog which would later also include a formal acknowledgment of the ways I believed I had been wrong.

Through these pages you will find not only my open-hearted and extensive personal process, but also a serious in depth apology unlike any that has been written before by anyone who was in leadership within the culture of what has been known as ex-gay ministry.

I will also share with you the dramatic transition I am going through that has brought waves of questions and shock to those involved in the communities that I served for over two decades.

It is my greatest desire that the readers may find acknowledgment for their pain, but also freedom from shame that remains a barrier to moving on into a life of true freedom. Throughout this book, you will see a progression of thought, process and changes within my belief system and faith. I hope you choose to follow along with me on my very personal journey.

PART ONE

A Shocking Picture

January 2012

"Give me wisdom and knowledge, that I may lead this people, for who is able to govern this great people of yours?" (2 Chronicles 1:10)

"Between The Purpose That Once Was—And The Unknown" (Kevyn Bashore)

Cameron Street, Steelton, PA

Wednesday, September 21, 2011

iPhone 4 Camera, Hipstamatic

www.kevynbashore.com

The ominous and decaying building behind this fire hydrant is crumbling under its own weight. But there's a beauty in its design and structure that can still be viewed by passersby. One can only imagine that the fire hydrant that once stood as a miniature guardian to protect this once thriving building from fire is now protecting something that the owners would probably celebrate if it burned down. The purpose of this hydrant has disintegrated amidst the peeling paint and wood.

What do we do when our purpose, the thing we've lived our life for, the thing we've passionately pursued, the thing we've lived and breathed for years, maybe decades, is removed or taken from our grasp? Many respond with anger, fear, grief. Some grow lethargic. Others hopeless. Some choose to end their lives over a loss of direction and purpose.

I wonder if anyone is protected from experiencing such loss at least once in their life? Some people appear impervious to such hardships. Others seem to be caught in a never-ending cycle of loss and despair. But to survive such disorientation and pain, one must experience renewal, sometimes in body, soul, and spirit, before catching a glimpse of a new vision and purpose to pursue in life.

Here's to all those who feel like the fire hydrant in today's photo. May you be renewed and grasp a passionate hope that will propel you into your destiny. (As written by Kevyn Bashore about his piece of art.)

Wow, what a shocking picture! Well, maybe not for some. It is actually a beautiful capture of life. I've developed a great appreciation for photographic artists and often affirmed their artistic gift to us this way. Photographic artists put a frame around everyday life so that I can enjoy the intimate beauty that I otherwise would have missed.

Kevyn Bashore has been working on a "365 – day" I-Phone photo project. After coming across his project through FaceBook, I began looking over some of his pictures, this one struck me deeply. Then I read what he had written about his creation.

As I looked at the picture I was mindful of how many years I was invested in ex-gay ministry. I lived and breathed its life, message, story, and purpose. In many ways, I was the "fire hydrant" protector of its image, reputation, and mission. I stood in the gap many times when it appeared to be threatened. There were those times when I felt my purpose was to take care of any flames that might roar.

Some of you may have been following my story, my writing, and have been hearing some very deep things from my heart. Thank you for listening.

For over two decades, I held invisible swords against the enemies of Love in Action, Exodus International, and the ex-gay culture. I remember meetings where I defended strongly the history, the nostalgia and many of the artifacts that represented the heritage of these organizations. I took the role of being a steward of the generations of its life.

When I was leaving my post at Love In Action, I diligently created a list of all the things that were significant to its years of existence. Things that rested on the walls, the floors, and the storage rooms of the ministry were always something I felt a need to protect. I feared if I didn't create a document with information of the origins and significance that it would all be lost and no one would know what they were and remember them as I did. I gave that document to numerous people that seemed to be left in charge after my departure with the hope that someone would take it seriously and take over my burden.

I feverishly scanned teaching material, informational books, literature and any other documents to protect them in the event that they would be taken by fire, or even more fearful, destroyed by someone who didn't care about them anymore. I was a self-made guardian.

Today, I am not so sure I feel the same sense of stewardship for those things. The real issue at hand for me personally isn't so much about the things mentioned. But due to many changes in my perspective, I am digging even more deeply into my heart. Questions loom like: What is my heart's desire? What am I passionate about? Or even a question that feels threatening as I move through my fifties, "What will the last season of my life look like?"

As I looked at the fire hydrant in the picture, I saw myself as a strong, mighty, landmark of purpose. Yes, with my hands tightly clenched, ready to aim toward the enemy, I was needed. I had a sense of worth. I was the mighty hero for many people who wanted me to be the strong stable one who would never stop or move away. I pictured myself as an old man still in position. Funny thing, before I chose to resign, some of my friends were casting lots to see if John Smid would ever leave Love In Action!

Looking at the house in the picture, I realized that I don't have the same passion to protect it any longer. Like the house, my role with this former ministry has lagged in my heart. My purposes of old have gone away. There isn't anything to protect any longer. Then the question becomes, What am I to do now? Or even more challenging, Who am I now? Or, What do I want to be now?

Thirty years ago, something dramatic occurred within my life. Prior to becoming an active Christian I had no purpose, seemingly no skills, no real gift to mankind. I felt invisible, and unnecessary. But when I discovered a tangible faith in God, it seemed that everything I put my hand to became a significant role for me to play within its structure or program.

First, in the spring of 1984, I was the founder and director for Clowns Created by Christ, a pantomime clown outreach ministry. It grew, people became involved and passionate with me as we clowned around within our faith community. Then soon I became a front-end guy for F.O.C.A.S, a vibrant Christian singles ministry. Then I was invited to become part of the Executive Committee for that same ministry. I attended singles ministry leadership conferences and saw potential of further involvement there.

My direction changed when I discovered ex-gay ministries in the summer of 1986 and went on staff with Love In Action as a House Leader for their residential community. Just a year later, I became the office manager, responsible for most of the office functions. Then within four years, September of 1990, I was asked to become the Director for the entire ministry. The next summer I was elected to the Board of Directors for Exodus International, a national coalition for ex-gay ministries.

In many of the churches I have been involved with I have been considered one of the honorary staff members, being invited to staff meetings and planning events. No matter what I did, it seemed I found purpose, calling, and fulfillment in leadership roles. It seemed I had a place in life that was validated and it appeared others bore witness to the work I was doing. It all seemed so right, fulfilling, important, and certainly I gained accolades for how well I was doing. I was a very well known ex-gay. I appeared on numerous national broadcasts, interviews for many newspapers and stood at the pulpits of many churches. I looked as though I had fought the odds of the homosexual plight and had won.

My role as the fire hydrant in life was solidly in place, and it seemed nothing could move it, nor did anyone want it moved. To remove something as profoundly protective as the fire hydrant is a very threatening thing to consider. What if there is a need—then what?

As I pondered the picture of the fire hydrant and the words of my friend, I went where my mind and heart never wanted to go before. I began to wonder what would happen if John Smid simplified his current life, found a cozy place by a stream with a wonderfully comfortable chair, and just rested? Would the earth rock off of its axis? Would someone's life end? Would MY life end?

A couple of years ago an acquaintance posed a question for me to consider. "John, what is your heart's desire?"

Actually, I had no answer for him, and as I read the question in his email, I actually found my mind going into a frizzle! I didn't want to think about that question at all! So I put it on the back burner, but never out of my mind.

I always found a way to forge forward into whatever purpose or plan seemed to be in front of me. I would find a calling, a significance and affirmation somewhere. I would be OK without answering the question, because isn't my heart's desire ministry, prophetic ministry? Haven't I always wanted that? Isn't that what God created me for?

After my first breath as a baby Christian, seemingly that is where I've been! Yes, prophetic ministry where I proclaimed hope for those burdened in their lives. I was a public spokesperson to stand for whatever I felt strongly laid upon my heart. It was well-known that John Smid would have something to say, an agenda to challenge, or at least a proclamation of right and wrong!

So, the plaque is falling from my heart a little at a time. For the first time in a very long time, I am open to pondering the question, What is my heart's desire?

Oh, man, where will this lead me? Am I willing to let it all go and just move towards my heart's desire—whatever that may be? I was talking with a good friend this week and I began to look around the world I have created for myself. I live in a wonderful large home, having a nice place to entertain. I have a closet full of clothes, many of which I don't even wear. I love my garden. I have a home office that many would drool over, full of my own memorabilia and ministry tools. But do any of them really make me happy? Do I need them for fulfillment?

I realized I have surrounded myself with things that support my purposes. The infrastructure of pipes, valves, water sources all support the fire hydrant. They are all necessary as long as the hydrant is in place that will be used in case of emergency. But what if the house goes away and the neighborhood is no longer anything other than a pile of dirt? What then will happen to the fire hydrant? If it is removed, then what's the purpose for the pipes and valves? They are no longer needed and therefore will rust away unless they are removed.

That is the way I began to look at the things that surround the life of John Smid. If I allow my heart's desire to be revealed and it isn't the life I now live, then what value do all of these things have? Would I need a large home? Many of the clothes in my closet could be given away and not even missed. The office full of papers, tools, supplies, could be dispersed and no one would know they were gone.

What is the support system of our life supporting? Is it our heart's desire, or is it just busyness personified? Have I been a master at distraction these last 30 years? Have I succeeded in developing an internal denial system with things and ministry purposes? Have I been distracting myself from my very own heart's desire not wanting to acknowledge what may lie underneath?

And where do I want to go from here? Do I want to continue to try be a fire hydrant for a cause or a ministry? Does God need me to be His fire hydrant? Or do I want to find true Sabbath rest within my Savior that isn't at all dependent on what I do for Him, but rather who I am in Him?

For years I have taught that God's love for us would not change even if we sat on our duffs for the rest of our lives here on earth. But do I believe that for myself? What if I find a cabin in the woods, simplify my life and just rest? Will that be OK with God? Will I be OK with that? Is it OK, just to rest? Or, do I need to be busy for the Kingdom to feel accepted, loved and affirmed? Should I stop and smell the roses? Do I take time to enjoy? Should I get out of the clatter and clanging of life and see what is really in my heart? Or is that all still too scary to even think about?

What about your life? Do you live on a treadmill of maintenance based on a false front, or a busy hero lifestyle? Do you want to avoid the question, "What is your heart's desire?" Are you living in an artificial environment where your life feels like a runaway train and you can't seem to stop it? Do you believe the wheels would fall off if you stopped? Do you continue to maintain your kingdom without seeing the purpose has really changed?

Thank you, Kevyn Bashore, for capturing the beauty of the Fire Hydrant and the house. Your creative genius has deeply affected my life.

Love In Action

Founded 1973

Love in Action was formed in 1973 when a small group of people and a pastor began to meet to find a way to encourage and support people who had admitted they were gay and struggling with their faith.

This group grew into a formal ministry that began to respond to letters nationwide that came from struggling men and women seeking answers. The first director, Frank Worthen, had developed a cassette tape with his testimony of salvation and that he had left the bondage of homosexuality. This was called the Brother Frank Testimony.

During the mid seventies a movement called The Jesus Movement was very strong in California. There were Christian houses for single and married people to live together while discovering their newly found faith in Christ. The Church of the Open Door facilitated several of these houses within their church congregation. Love In Action staff and the pastors of this church decided that it might be a good thing to develop a Christian house for gay people seeking support and encouragement. This was the beginning of Love In Action's live-in program.

The ministry to homosexuals was a brand new concept. This is largely because in 1973 the American Psychological Association had removed homosexuality from their Diagnostics and Statistical Manual as a disorder. The Christian community saw this as an opposing decision from their understanding that homosexuality is a sin, and therefore must continue to be taught as such. Therefore ministries began to crop up around the country to defeat this decision, considered to be a liberal decision of secular humanism.

As Love In Action grew to be more well known, their residential program grew as well. After a few years it became a full one year program of teaching and supportive groups. There were two houses and a third house had just been developed in 1986. This is where I came to California to be on staff. They needed a house leader for their New Hope House.

I was an outsider that had a fresh look at the structure of their houses and shortly became their director for House Ministries. In this position I was given the opportunity to change some things and add new teaching materials to their spectrum of lectures. I was also helping to bring new structure to hopefully help make the outcome better.

At this point the men and women who came to the program held full time jobs during the day, and had two groups each week in the evenings. One group was a teaching group, the other was a book study or a group discussion. The bulk of the real work occurred within the relationships of those who lived together in the houses. The house leaders were the main counselors unless something more significant was needed, then Frank Worthen would be brought in to help.

One man, who had been a pastor, came into the program who had a serious dilemma. He was married and was having numerous sexual encounters outside of his marriage. His wife laid down the law that he must live faithful to her or he would lose his marriage. Our staff got together and devised a plan to help keep him from acting upon his sexual urges. We would establish an accountability structure where he could never be alone. He had to be with at least one or two others at all times.

This was the beginning of developing a more specific model of ministry that was similar to other programs for addiction such as alcohol, or chemical dependency. The man was thankful for the help and felt safe from the threat of losing his marriage. He successfully ended his one year program without acting out and we all saw this as a victory.

The structures for our program became more rigid as we thought we would see even more success from our program. It was then that we became a premier program for men and women to come to receive help or counseling. Since the majority of other ministries were basically support groups, Love In Action was the place to send those who had serious problems with addictive sex. But along with those referrals, we also received men and women who were just seeking the premier program with the thought that we had the goods to help them.

Our program was set up as a cost program. Meaning we just charged enough to cover the cost of what we were doing and at that time, the fees were about $500 per month for living expenses and the counseling program. Frank Worthen took no salary, and never did after that. So myself and the Office Manager were the only paid staff. Our expenses were kept to the minimum and we often had to struggle just to pay for a copying machine and postage meter.

Frank Worthen resigned from the ministry to begin a mission outreach in Manila, Philippines. At that point I was appointed to the position of Director. I had been there for four years and felt challenged, but confident that I could take it further. We added more structure, and application filters to make decisions about who would come into the program. We went through a stringent process of prayer, reading, and evaluation of the applicants. We even kept the pictures out of the applications during the initial evaluation so as to not have a bias based on physical appearance. We truly thought we were effective in the selection process and received each new client with joy and acceptance.

In just a couple of years, our program increased in size so much that we were overwhelming our small church in Marin County, California.

After much discussion we decided to move the program. We searched for a place to plant ourselves and finally a church in Memphis Tennessee invited us to move and come under their support. It was a very large church of about 3000 people so we believed they could absorb our ministry.

After our move we continued for a short season with the model of clients working full time and evening groups. It seemed to work well and helped the clients to pay for their fees which by this time had increased to $950 per month. This was due to that fact that we no longer had a self supporting Director and had added four more paid staff members. The costs in Memphis for housing decreased, but other expenses increased for computers, copiers, staff, and administration. Our program was now a nationwide model and sought after for much input and counsel from other ministries. By this time several other live-in programs had developed and saw us as mentors for their staff and structure.

In 2000 we moved into a wonderful new space with the counselor that was acting as our clinical supervisor. We were allowed to customize our offices and meeting rooms to wonderful specifications. We believed we had finally found an increase in stability as we had a 10 year verbal agreement with the owner.

When we saw the culture changing and there was a decrease in enrollment we sought outside counsel for how to match the changing times. It was at this point we developed our new program called The Source. We changed everything over to the new model in 2001. This new structure was a ninety day program with daytime groups. The clients didn't work a full time job and we believed it would be better since they could focus on their program full time for a shorter amount of time. We saw enrollment increase and our program was full again. The fees for The Source were $7000 for three months. We also offered a shorter program of one month for $2500.

In 2002 we went through one of the worst financial droughts we had ever been through. We had no idea how we were going to remain afloat!

During this serious time, the owner of the building went awol and left us to manage the full cost of the building. We couldn't pay the rental agreement and could barely pay the utilities. After a few months, the family of the landlord put the building up for sale and we lost our space and were left with a tremendous debt we had incurred to remodel the space.

We moved into a temporary office that barely accommodated our needs and we became a happy family living closely together sharing offices and bumping into each other regularly. Our program grew to the highest enrollment we had seen in many years. Each day we were feeding 25 people out of a small butler's type of office kitchen. But we strove to continue to be the best we knew how to be.

We had outside support groups through the years for families and individuals. But we finally were able to hire a full time community outreach coordinator. His personality and talents led us to have the largest community group ministry we had ever had. Everything seemed to be going extremely well.

We had become one of the few ex-gay ministries that had credentials that the world would deem appropriate for a ministry like ours which boosted our confidence and we started seeking licensed counselors to further boost the confidence in what we had to offer.

In 2004 we began to search for a building that would offer further growth and take us to the next level of success. After a long search we found a small church campus that was for sale for a very reasonable price. It had three buildings on five acres with 20,000 square feet of space. It was an amazing shift for us. We now had a full commercial kitchen, two large meeting rooms, administrative offices, a 350 seat auditorium and a small chapel. We thought surely this would bring us even more clients, since we had the room, and further credibility through owning our own campus.

During the last season that I was the director of Love In Action, each day was very full for me and for each client. The clients lived in two individual homes that were owned by the ministry. The residential component was a major factor in the life of the program. The clients had to learn how to live in community with all of the twists and turns of relationships. Involvement in a local church each Sunday was a part of the weekly routine for outside input and perspective. When they returned home each evening from the ministry campus they had to prepare a dinner meal, and maintain the cleaning and maintenance of their home. The rotation schedule and management of the home was facilitated by our residential House Managers. Their job was one of the toughest that any of us had because they dealt with the real stuff in the relationships with the clients and they had to maintain a healthy atmosphere within the home environment.

Each morning on campus began with a chapel that was taught by a staff member or a local ministry leader or pastor. The daily schedule also consisted of several lectures and at least one or two discussion groups every day. There were weekly activities that were facilitated like volunteering at a local food distribution project at a local church. Staff counselors would move in and out of groups and one on one sessions with the clients.

Along with teaching five or more sessions each week, I was also personally responsible for maintaining the donations, financial structure, and administrative components of the ministry. I had to make sure to maintain our five acre campus and two residential homes and I had an ongoing schedule of speaking engagements, many of which were out of town which kept me busy on many weekends. At the peak of our ministry, around 2005, we had fifteen full time staff members, 26 clients, and numerous volunteers and an annual budget of $700,000.

There were also four family conferences that we hosted each year with an average attendance of around 80 people at each one. Needless to say, managing a full time residential program was a heavy load to carry. I had done this for so many years it became natural for me. But that didn't remove the pressure of making sure it all worked together and was adequately funded.

It was at this point in June of 2005 that we were struggling with internal staff breakdowns and a protest that came on the very first day of holding groups on our new campus. This was the beginning of huge changes in our ministry, and little did I know, huge changes in my own life.

As you read through the following pages, you will find a chronological series of blogs that will reveal these changes as I moved through this challenging transition.

(Note: In 2012, Love In Action officially changed its name to Restoration Path Ministry.)

I Don't Trust You

Spring 2005

The following situation brought about the first outward sign that something was changing deep within my heart. A dramatic shift was about to occur, but I had no clue what I would go through as the challenging years to come would shake loose virtually every foundation of my former years.

Something was different this Monday morning. A new mercy, an opening of my ears, and a sense of peace and patience came over me. I thought back over the last several months and found I had a new battle to be won! A battle for grace, a battle for compassion for others. After so many years of being the truth speaker and the one who was often called to strongly confront wrong behavior, my role was about to change dramatically. This was the beginning of a new era of life for me, but I didn't see what was ahead of me.

"My dear friends, if you know people who have wandered from God's truth, don't write them off. Go after them. Bring them back, and you will have rescued precious lives from destruction and prevented an epidemic of wandering away from God." James 5:19-20 (The Message)

Earlier this year a very good friend had confessed that he had gotten himself tangled up in some addictive behavior. I knew this wasn't the first time and that he had been into this and my heart sank with despair and fear. He was a part of a family that we had grown to love dearly. We laughed together, cried together, carried moving boxes together and considered each other close as if we were family. Actually, in Christ, we were.

As he spoke of more details concerning the situation, I felt my skin turn ghostly white. What would I do this time? I asked myself if this meant that I might lose this friendship forever. Would our relationship survive such a devastation? Our lives had become so close I wondered how many other ways we would be affected by this unfortunate circumstance.

This was overwhelming to me but with a new and strange reaction. I felt compelled to stand by my friend because I knew his heart. He had a heart of love for God, for his wife, and for his family. I knew he needed someone to believe in him; but I kept thinking, "Can I ever trust him again?" Then I thought about the concept of trust and why I was so determined to have that question answered.

We had decided to meet for coffee to talk as we had so often before. This time I found myself motivated by commitment to the relationship rather than to spend time with a friend. I remember speaking from my heart and saying, "I don't trust you!" I felt smug about my statement because somehow I felt I needed to take some kind of stand against what he was doing to harm himself. I perceived I had to draw some kind line in the sand. I thought my statement would keep this in perspective. After all, I thought I had to be able to trust him in order to be his friend. But what did trust mean? How would it be applied?

Why did I have to trust him? I couldn't control his behavior. I couldn't control his remorse or his current or future choices. I could however choose to make healthy personal choices for myself, so why was it so important for me to trust him? Sadness came over me again as I thought about the process that I was going through, and I grieved over what had happened.

In my evaluation of the concept of trust, I realized that much of my need to trust my friend had to do with my own personal needs and had little to do with him. I thought I had to be able to trust him so that I wouldn't be hurt again. In the end, my need to trust was really a desire to control my demand that he be trustworthy! It was all about me. I was trying to reach an impossible goal of manipulating my friend to behave so that we could have a relationship. I wanted him to mind his p's and q's and not repeat this again! I needed something from him as a friend, and his behavior had threatened getting what I needed in this relationship.

When I was sitting with him at a local coffee shop, I looked at him. He was weak, sad, needy, and broken. He had always been so positive and encouraging. I was used to sharing my life with him to gain support for my own weakness and life struggles, but this day was different. He had nothing to give me; he was empty. I made a decision that day.

He was my confidant. But now, he had his own troubles and I knew I needed to utilize other friends to lean on. I knew I couldn't talk with him about personal stuff because of his weakened state, but I could listen to him and bear his burdens. He was doing everything he could to stay alive and make it through this current devastation. He needed me much more than I needed him. I had other friends and places for support. At this time, he had been abandoned by so many others due to their responses to his circumstances. There were few available for him to lean on.

I realized that I no longer needed to trust him. This was so freeing for me to accept. I was able to release him to his own choices. I let him go to either succeed or fail, but my life was no longer dependent upon his being good or obedient or safe. I drew some healthy boundaries around my heart so that he was free to live his life as he chose to.

That day, I chose to enter into his pain and share it with him. I made the decision to listen to his heart and to watch and wait for whatever the Lord wanted to do with him. It was between him and God alone. I would just be his friend and cry with him in his pain, and rejoice in the restoration if that came about. I was hopeful that this would be the case but no longer demanded that it be so.

Well, hallelujah! Today, his life is restored. Our friendship is different. There are scars, but there is also more peace and relief overall. We have shared the common bond of a battle for his life and he lived. If I encounter something terribly disheartening, I hope there will be someone there for me who releases me to God.

In a recent phone call my friend was deep in the middle of some more growth battles. This time they weren't from bad choices, but from good ones. He had made further choices to enter into the risks of life to pursue his passions, his family, and his Lord. When he answered the phone, he told me how much of a challenge the week had been. He described that he was in the middle of mud up to his knees in a cattle yard, trying to get through the day. I let go of my properness and said to him, "It seems you are in a deep pile of sh%$#". He began to cry; then his sobbing turned into laughter.

We both got a good belly laugh out of our short phone call that day. Those tears and that laughter didn't come from just the current circumstances but from a lifetime of living through terror and joy with Jesus. I don't need to control my friend's behavior anymore because his life is in the Lord's hands as is my life.

> Live creatively, friends. If someone falls into sin, forgivingly restore him, saving your critical comments for yourself. You might be needing forgiveness before the day is out. Stoop down and reach out to those who are oppressed. Share their burdens, and so complete Christ's law. If you think you are too good for that, you are badly deceived. Gal 6:1-3 (The Message)

The Protest!

June 2005

June 6, 1944, is remembered for D-Day and the invasion of France. That day marked the convergence of two hemispheres, the battle of two lifestyles, and a clash between two kinds of men. It was a result of many years of experience, building up an army, planning and preparation. This was a deciding moment in world history. The memorable conflict was the beginning of the end of World War II.

Sixty-one years later to the day, I thought a lot about D-day. Right outside my office window, there was a theater of war on the sidewalk and passionate words were being projected over the megaphone which seemed as loud as the cannons on Omaha Beach. Personal convictions clashed without a personal exchange and in our own way we were fighting for what each of us felt was right.

We were against each other, but we were not communicating with each other. It almost appeared as if one of us was speaking French and the other English.

Culture wars! It seems that most battles have always been about shifts in culture or between people who perceive cultural changes will negatively impact their very foundation of life. This battle wasn't any different.

A new beginning! A fresh start. It was the very first day we were in our newly purchased building in the Raleigh area just outside Memphis, Tennessee. The vision of a new place to work was very present in my mind when the staff arrived early that morning. We were all excited to be there and enjoy the culmination of a plan we had seen come to fruition.

In my mind, the plan was to quietly move into the new facility, and the neighborhood. I didn't even want to place the name of the organization on a sign out front when we moved in so as to not draw attention to our presence. In my mind, I just wanted to be a neighbor, not an issue.

"John Smid! Where are you, John?" the bullhorn blared. With the quiet joy of being in our new building violently interrupted, I felt embarrassed by the public display and fearful that the neighbors would become upset by the interruption of their lives too. This was a conservative older neighborhood after all.

Down on the street in front of a large church-like campus was a stream of people. Holding colorful flags and signs with passionate expressions, they moved with strong conviction that something had gone terribly wrong. One man holding a video camera seemed to be organizing them as he recorded their every move. The cameraman was wearing a head scarf and looked like he was on the fringe, considering the midsouthern culture. He seemed to believe that the event needed to be recorded and was making sure that occurred.

I was the visionary desirous of a fresh start, and yet I shuddered with confusion and questions. "Why are all of these people here? What do they want with me?" I had no idea as to what had inspired them to gather for such a passionate show of conviction. The shock of what I was faced with upset my entire world that day almost as though a bomb had gone off right in the middle of the building.

They were yelling out a young man's name from the street. They were saying things like: "Zack, we're here for you." "You're not alone." It was extremely odd all the way around. It was as though someone needed to be rescued from some terrible impending harm!

"There are protesters outside!" someone yelled. Unprepared for this attack, inside the building we were scurrying around in an attempt to find out more about what was happening on the street. The phones began to ring from news stations, the national media, and emails started to come in like a flood. Much like in 1944 when radios reported the breakout of D-Day, the internet ran hot with reactions to the events on that street corner in 2005.

What could have possibly been that important? What kind of things were going on that would cause an entire nation—the world even—to respond to what was happening at Love In Action on June 6, 2005?

Freedom. It was a battle over freedom. Freedom to do what? Or freedom from what? The man with the signature head scarf wanted freedom for the young man inside. I was also passionate to defend the young man's freedom. So, what were they fighting about? Didn't they want the same thing for him that I did?

These men were very invested in their views of freedom. The crowd wanted to fight for the young man's rights to live as he sees fit. They perceived that the folks under the steeple were brainwashing, controlling, and holding individuals captive.

But those that were their focus were only 16 and 17 years old! Their parents had brought them here desiring to help them. They thought they might have been harmful to themselves if they continued down a path of social or relational connections they believed to be wrong. I was there to help too. I believed in freedom to choose as well. But I also believed that in order to make healthy choices in life these young people needed to experience some things that might help them make those choices.

Morgan Fox was the man with the camera in hand, wearing the head scarf. He appeared to be directing the crowd. I had never met Morgan, or any of the protestors for that matter. We had never had a conversation, nor had we ever been in the same room at the same time. The relationship gap was huge. There had been no communication between us to listen, to hear or understand what was really happening that day.

The streets were wild with honking cars and trucks, cameras, newsmen, and protestors. The driveways to the ministry property were crowded with people who had gathered along with Morgan. They truly believed a young man's life was in danger. The intensity was extreme, and no one had any clarity about what was at the root of all of the mayhem.

Several young teens were in a daytime program that was scheduled to meet for two weeks. Among them was Zach, who had earlier posted on his MySpace blog that his parents were sending him to an ex-gay camp. His entry was seen by some friends and it went viral!

The protestors decided they would return with cameras in hand each morning and evening when the teenagers would come and go from the building. "What do we do now?" the staff wondered. How can we manage this outcry for social justice? We love these kids and know there is hope for freedom from what we had believed to be their addictive behaviors.

Morgan and the crowd believed they were right too. Certainly they believed they could help Zach find freedom from religious oppression. On the other hand, as a ministry, Love In Action believed they could help him to know the freedom they had found from hormones and lusts that we believed would become harmful. The tug of war was huge for the rights of this young man inside and outside the building.

It was a battle over homosexuality. The rights and wrongs of this issue have drawn culture wars for years. Morgan and I were on two sides of the fence in passionate response to the same issue. Our definitions of freedom were dramatically different—or were they? We didn't know the answer to that question because we had never talked. We had never heard each other's hearts. We had never communicated.

Introduced to one another through an emotional crowd with a megaphone, there was no place that day to listen. It didn't appear that any agreement would be reached anytime soon! Morgan and I needed a map, a path to each other's hearts. But how would we find that in the middle of the battle of June 6, 2005?

The Impact Continues

Summer 2005

Those on the street didn't show any interest in hearing my heart. Their agenda was to shout their convictions thinking that whatever was going on in that church would stop! I wasn't interested in hearing their heart either. They were a huge interruption and I just wanted them to be gone.

While it didn't show that day, I believe that one of the most effective models of communicating love for one another is through genuine relationships. This kind of love comes out naturally as we hear one another's hearts and value one another's created purpose for life.

The passion Morgan and I felt that day was driven by our deeply invested convictions. The chasm between us didn't allow our feelings to come out in ways that would be understood. The walls of the building and the distance from the sidewalk were barriers to even the thought of talking with each other, much less building a relationship. There was no interest in knowing each other because we felt so entitled to being right.

It is my greatest hope that people know they are loved by God. As I write these words I feel embarrassed about the lack of application of things that I believed in so strongly. Out of my own fears I allowed my convictions to be lost. I intentionally kept my distance from the conflictive actions on the street. I wanted to just ignore them and pretend they were just protestors rather than acknowledge their personhood.

In the end, one of the main purposes of my walk on earth is to be a representative of the grace of God to others; I really desire to be someone who will be a messenger of His unconditional love.

During the months following that protest in 2005, a huge transition occurred in my life. In order to honestly evaluate the conflicts between Morgan and me, there had to be a change from the inside. The external judgments and intentional alienation from him were dishonest and built on years of being set in my ways thinking that I was right and certainly whoever disagreed must be wrong.

One bright sunny unsuspecting morning an officer of the law showed up at our ministry door. "John, we have a report that there is abuse of a minor occurring here. We'd like to speak with the young man." I was instructed to never release a person's identity and this seemed to be a great time to pull out the manual on professional boundaries. "I'm sorry, sir, but I can neither confirm nor deny anyone's presence here." I quickly went to call a lawyer and get instruction on this matter. He told me I had to divulge the information to the officer. When I returned, the officer let me know that he understood what was happening here and that he wanted to get this over as quickly as possible so that it didn't get out of hand. I felt a sense of ease that he was actually trying to help us so I was able to relax.

Just a month or so later we had another knock at our door, it was the alcohol and drug counseling license authorities. They were there to respond to a complaint that we were facilitating a drug and alcohol addiction program without a license. I assured them that was not what we were doing and explained that we had a licensed drug counselor on staff but he was just there to relate to those who came to us that had struggles with chemical dependency. They were satisfied that we were

NOT an official drug program and another sigh of relief came out of my chest.

But, the larger challenge came a little later. The health department approached us with the charge that we were running a residential mental health program that MUST be licensed or they would shut down the ministry and lock the doors. I had now hit the limit of what I was prepared to handle. After calling all the resources I could think of we entered into an all out battle with the health department of Tennessee.

With the help of some powerful attorneys, we were advised to file a law suit against the State of Tennessee for the misapplication of the law, and violation of our First Amendment Rights as a faith based organization.

About a year later, we won the law suit but not without a tremendous amount of stress. We were released from the allegations. The fees of over $70,000 were fortunately absorbed by the non-profit legal firm and ordered to be repaid by the State of Tennessee. But, our reputation as a ministry was in shambles.

The Church

June 2006

I spent many years of my Christian life sitting in pews and church buildings. But honestly, I hadn't really learned what to do outside of those walls. At the time after the protest settled down, for the first time in many years, God inspired me to a renewed desire to reach out to others sharing His love with them.

I began to pray, seeking God for a plan. What did He want me to do with what He had shown me? So, for four years, I prayed. I sorted through my varied responses, some not so pretty to talk about. I began to wrestle with my vocational life. I had been in the same ministry for over twenty years. I was really satisfied in what I had done, but something began to shift causing me to reevaluate my daily investments in my work.

I've read through some books on missional churches, organic churches, and house churches and found some great inspiration through them, but there seemed to be something still missing. Some of these books were tremendous and liberating in my heart, but at times they left me feeling frustrated and critical. I had to continue working through that too. It seemed they were just another kind of church program that didn't look that much different from where I had been.

God began to rock my world through adversity and relational challenges that had been erupting inside the ministry walls as well as surrounding the churches I had been a part of. I began to experience shifting in every area of my life. I had no idea how tough things were going to get, and I am so grateful that God took me through it all gradually.

From 1999, I was a part of an organized church that was a tremendous blessing for thousands who attended its services. After a horrible internal breakdown in June of 2006, two-thirds of the congregation, including my wife and me, along with the majority of the staff including the senior pastor walked out the door. Literally thousands were deeply wounded. The very next Sunday I organized a gathering in a local park to celebrate Father's Day. That Sunday was one of the best church services I had remembered in some time.

I began to visit other churches sporadically, almost feeling relieved that I didn't attend an organized church every Sunday morning.

I remember one Sunday sitting on my cool breezy front porch wondering if this pleased the Lord for me to just be quiet with Him instead of going out to a church that day. It was almost as though God laughed. I thought this surely was liberation from being bound to a pattern of church attendance that had raised me to more maturity but also brought me a lot of pain.

We settled into a small home study group from our former church. There were about sixteen people who were fast becoming really close friends. I started to ask the question about whether this would replace the larger organized church for me and others. Most of the time this weekly Saturday night gathering meant more to me than a majority of formal organized church services I had attended in recent years.

We met together every week, ate a meal, and studied the Bible together, supporting and encouraging each other with prayer and counsel. We surrounded each other at weddings, funerals, and hospital stays. We ate other meals together sometimes and I had spontaneous lunches with the men. I affectionately called it my church of sixteen members and twelve regular attendees.

But there was still something conflictive about not going to a regular church. I found another local church that seemed to have something special, and I knew some friends who had been going there and said they enjoyed it. I happened to meet a couple at a home cookout who went there and they invited us to attend, so we went the next day.

I resigned myself that maybe this might become what we needed and would enjoy. The new church gathering of Christians very quickly embraced us. I was invited to speak and share my gifts with the body there. The pastor was very supportive of me personally and spoke into my life with renewed encouragement. So we joined this church with the hope in our hearts that we would find a special ministry there and relationships that were fulfilling.

During this season another very deeply invested part of my life became a huge challenge. The internal workings of Love In Action, the ministry I had led for over twenty years became broken, confusing, and wounding. I tried every way I knew how to correct the problems. I prayed, sought intercession and counsel, but things continued to worsen.

The conflicts and distractions increased, and I felt trapped in a place I had celebrated for so many years. I hated leaving my home every day to go to a place that was such a personal and corporate challenge for everyone. What was God doing? How could it be like this? It seemed no matter which way I turned, I couldn't find a solution.

I began to search God's heart for some answers. This time I began to ask different questions than before. I pondered questions that would take me deeper than just asking what organized church to attend. God, what is Your church? Where is Your church? What does it mean to serve You? How do I fit into Your church? Who is Your church? God, where do You want me to be?

After a couple of years of tremendous heartache from all of the conflicts, in 2008 I left my position with Love In Action. I believed that God had something He was leading me to. I realized that one of the first answers He gave me was to free me from the ministry I led. It became very clear that God was allowing me to close the door on that season of my life and begin anew. I felt strongly that He wanted me to take all I had learned and experienced there and use it in a new way.

Upon my departure from Love In Action, my pastor invited me to share a teaching series with a small group at church. I called it The Tributaries of Grace. I started out the series inviting the participants to focus on a person they wanted to reach with the grace of God. This could have been a friend, a family member, or someone they were having a difficult time with. As I challenged this small group to reach out, I thought about Morgan. After all, he had upset my whole world and caused endless problems, but we had begun to meet and get to know one another so I wondered where this would lead?

Something new came alive in my heart. I realized that through the years of ministry experience I mostly responded to those desiring healing and recovery from homosexuality. This had changed to looking outwardly into the lives of those who might be searching for a connection, or reconnection with God. So there was a glimpse of a major change in my perspective at that point. I couldn't get my mind off of those within the gay community. I knew them. I am one of them. Who will reach those who are seeking a deeper walk with God?

Just when I finally let my guarded heart open to some extent, I began to feel released to step into further commitment with the people at the new church. But as I got further involved, I heard rumblings of discontent and elder/pastor problems that seemed to have been developing over a period of months.

One Sunday morning, we went through a painful and confusing combustion of problems within the organizational leadership. That day there was a split. The elders and staff resigned, leaving the pastor and about one half of the original congregation in the wake.

I left on that overwhelming Sunday feeling lost and hurt, realizing that many of my new friends were going different directions. Many of the departing members quickly reorganized and held a meeting within a couple of days announcing the beginning of a new church. What about the broken hearts from two days ago? How would they heal? Is anyone paying attention to the wounds that need mending? It had happened again. Now what? How many more times will we see this happen? I continued to wonder if there was any solution to these kinds of conflicts.

Needless to say, I was swimming in discouragement and hopelessness. What am I going to do now? What is God doing? I surely didn't want to attend any organized church the next week and decided to attach to our home group even more.

I released myself from Sunday church attendance obligations. I soon felt freer than I had been in a long time. After a few months, I felt God answer my questions in another very unique way. He said:

> "Watch for the springs of Living Water to come up out of the streets and sidewalks of the city. Get prepared! This water is the Living Water as unto salvation. I am inspiring my people to come to me and I want my Body to be prepared to receive them. But they will not be coming to the front doors of organized church buildings. They will need you to go to them, to listen for their voices, to know them and care about them. Go out into the streets."

Whoa! These many years of confusion and pain have brutally moved me to go outside the walls of the organized churches! Building by building God has seemingly jack hammered me loose from my own traditions, religious practice, and patterns of habit! He changed my entire world.

I began to see His church was everywhere I met or gathered with followers of Jesus Christ. I saw that I was having church every day! My new church didn't have physical walls, or membership other than to believe in Jesus Christ. I enjoyed lunches, spontaneous meetings in the market places of my life, which became encouraging connections with the Body of Christ. I found that when I took my eyes off of the Sunday ritual that had been a habit and somewhat of an idol, I saw the Body of Christ everywhere I went.

I have seen a new thing develop. I am now, more than at any time in my life, excited with the hope that I will see someone come to a relationship with God that is authentic, transforming, and invigorating! I have felt my eyes perk up in a watchful manner to see if I can see what He sees. There are lost children out there, Lord? Where are they? Do you want me to go to them? Where will I find them?

I felt Him saying, "You won't find them inside the walls of the churches. Walk as Jesus did, in the highways and byways, in the world around you. You will find them there."

Well, I have found myself in some really strange places! I have entered the world with weak knees, curiosity, and timidity. I didn't feel prepared for this! I was uncomfortable in the world. It was too strange for me. I wanted to be comfortable, safe, and this wasn't a safe place.

I was reminded that we don't live in a G-rated world. This world is not my home! But I am asked to enter it with my whole heart so as to be in it, but carefully—so as not to become entrenched in it.

Wow, this is really exciting—and dangerous. I have been around people and involved in circumstances that were similar to my own broken past, but I had forgotten my old life long ago. I have heard language, seen behavior, and gone places that many told me in the organized church I should not be around. I have lived in a whitewashed world sanitized in such a way that was designed to keep us safe from the world. Is that what Jesus did? What about the real grit of this world?

What about getting our hands really dirty—with the hope we will find the lost, the estranged, and the orphaned?

As I have gone through this journey of change, God has inspired me to write about what I am learning. Herein lays many of the words that have been inspired as a result of The Protest of 2005!

I believe that one of the greatest tools to bring hope to our world today is our own story, our own life. Like myself, I know others around me who hunger for connection and real relationship. So many are living lives of aloneness, fear, and shame that for some, the only way they will come out of their prisons will be to hold the hand of someone they trust. The trust will come from knowing that the other person can relate.

I found an answer to one of my questions, "What does it mean to serve the Lord?" It was simple and straightforward. To serve Him is to serve His people with His message of new life, hope, and healing. He wants us to never tire of speaking of the hope that is within us. Will we walk the streets of our lives with our hands outstretched, just like His were on the cross? Unafraid, unashamed, and ready to embrace, to hear, to value and honor, those we find there.

"Come to me, all you who are weary and burdened, and I will give you rest. Take my yoke upon you and learn from me, for I am gentle and humble in heart, and you will find rest for your souls." (Matthew 11: 28-29 NIV).

God, Just Surprise Me!

April 2008

As I continued to process leaving Love In Action I breathed a prayer, "God, I don't know what You want to do with me now. I want to make the next twenty years of my life count. I know You have brought me through a lot, and I have learned and grown so much in the last twenty years, so maybe You can use my experience to help someone else."

"I have no agenda, and I do not feel entitled to anything. I don't have a degree or a career track. I am not sure who would want to hire someone who has led an ex-gay ministry for most of my adult life. But I'm certain there is something in there that can be used. So I guess my greatest desire is for something radical, but I haven't a clue what that might be. So God, SURPRISE ME!"

My wife and I were on a Caribbean cruise in 2007. Our trip took us to a group of small islands called Turks and Caicos. When we got off the boat we met a lady who had just opened a horse and carriage ride to tour the island. As she spoke, she told us a little of the recent history of the island. She said that the island had been supported financially from a military base that was there. It appears it had recently been closed, and this had left the island financially broken. As I saw her business and the newly constructed Carnival Cruise Lines pier I could see some life coming back.

As we rode around the island on the carriage, our driver told us that the island was dependent on all outside resources for everything, including even the basic need of water. Their water had to be shipped in! This started my mind dreaming of all of the what ifs as I looked to my future.

What if God were to surprise me with a long-term trip to Turks and Caicos to begin a gospel outreach on the island? I cannot seem to get that thought out of my mind even today. What if God wanted to move us across the United States? I began to send out applications for pastoral positions around the country. I thought maybe someone could use my experience some way for the general populace of the church. I attempted to come up with a resume that would capitalize on my experiences.

I didn't get any call backs but still prayed for God's movement in finding a new career. I began a dialogue with the pastor of the church we attended. He immediately tried to encourage me and said that he may have a place in our church and we began to pray about that. He encouraged me to write a book and offered me a slot to teach something that was on my heart. He felt an urgency to keep me in the loop and to keep talking about what God was doing to prepare me for my future.

The teaching series I came up with I called Tributaries of Grace, based on a sermon that my pastor had given. I liked the thought of reaching into individual lives with a message of God's abundant love for them. Even though that was on my mind in June 2008, I had no idea of what this would mean later on. The series was a success. I had asked God for ten people, and He brought ten to the group. We were together for eight weeks.

I continued to pray about how I was going to make a living. I felt confident that God would provide and a little arrogant at the same time that I didn't have anything to worry about.

I Never Wanted to Know You

May 2008

I was alone a lot in my office and I had time to evaluate, to think, and to reestablish a new layer to my life. In the process I had many discussions along the way.

I was in a passionate conversation with a friend of mine about how each of us processed the issue of homosexuality. She began to talk about friends she had that were Christians and yet were involved in same-sex partnerships. I felt frustrated because she just didn't want to tell me what she thought about being for or against homosexual relationships. As we talked that day, seemingly for hours, I began to speak strongly about someone I had heard of for many years who was gay and claimed to be a Christian. Michael Bussee was one of the men who arranged the very first Exodus International conference.

Many years ago I watched a video in which Michael shared some of his life story, and I felt challenged by the things he was sharing. As I talked about Michael, I had disdain in my heart towards him. This led me to profile him with many others I judged to be rebellious and compromising of God's standards. I had never really wanted to know anyone who claimed to be a Christian but was living in an overt gay relationship. If they wanted help, they should say so; otherwise, I figured they would have to deal with God on these things and I kept my distance.

As I talked with Lisa, she got quiet. When I was done, she said, "John, don't you think it is unfair to form such strong opinions about someone you have never met? Don't you think you owe it to him to talk with him personally before you form an opinion about his character?"

Phew, That Was Humbling!

Lisa was absolutely right. I was unfair in basing my opinions about what I had heard rather than from my own experience with someone like Michael. I had a lot of Michaels in my life. I was smug in my heart regarding people like Michael. But for some reason I thought it was enough to gauge my opinions on what I had heard from others and didn't feel I needed to spend any time with them.

Lisa asked again, "John, would you be willing to talk with Michael? I can arrange a phone call if you are willing to hear his heart." What could I say? I had already crossed the line in what I had said about him. I at least owed him the respect to talk with him. Now I wondered if he were even willing to talk with me. After all, I am sure Michael had heard things about me through the years as well. I have no doubt that Michael was familiar with my involvement in ex-gay ministries, so I was sure he didn't think so favorably about me either. It was interesting to see how I went from "I don't want to talk with him" to "I wonder if he'll talk with me."

Lisa called me back and said Michael was willing to talk with me. We arranged a phone call, and I remember sitting in my office in a comfortable chair in preparation for the call. I was feeling nervous about the call. I wasn't sure what to expect in our conversation. So when the phone rang, I answered and after a little introductory conversation I was surprised at what transpired. We talked comfortably about our lives and experiences. Michael and I had a lot in common, both having been previously married and divorced. Michael went into a gay relationship and I went on to marry Vileen; but we had many shared experiences to talk about.

Michael Bussee became a person. I left the conversation feeling a sense of peace. I found Michael to be endearing, humble, honest, and very respectful of my life and experiences. He talked about some of the painful things he had experienced in his life as well as the joys. We related to having children and grandchildren as well. I felt a desire to talk with him again largely because he was a genuinely nice guy. He and I have formed a friendship that I respect as a person whose life matters and has value not only to God, but also to others as well.

It was now the summer of 2008 and I've now gone into more uncharted territory. I wondered what would come next. So I called Lisa and gave her my report, "Lisa, actually, I enjoyed talking with Michael." She said she had another friend she wanted me to talk with. She told me of a man named Todd Ferrell. She said he was someone she admired a lot and wanted me meet him. She connected us and we set a time to talk. I figured since Michael was a great guy maybe Todd would be someone that was nice too.

Todd and I decided to use Skype. After setting up my first Skype connection, we had a great time talking about our lives. Once again, I felt surprised at what I heard. Todd, like Michael, was sincere and willing to share pieces of his life that were filled with humility and honesty. Since I had never been in a friendship with someone that was gay affirming like Todd, I guess I expected to hear something different.

I was looking for excuses, like rationalizing Scripture to their own tastes. I was sure I would hear things that would offend me, but I found none of that. I am not sure what it was I expected, but I surely didn't expect to hear this!

"John, our church saw the pain in the gay community in San Francisco. As an outreach to bring Jesus to the streets, we decided to serve communion on Castro Street in San Francisco on Good Friday. There were requests for prayer, shared tears, and hunger for God that left us speechless. Yes, there were those who were on drugs, those who were angry, and other distractions. But in the end, we knew we had touched the hearts of many who were hungry to connect with God."

I was left in tears myself after hearing this story. "Todd, your heart beats the same as mine for the gay community. Of course, you know there are many evangelicals in our country that would think what your church did was blasphemous. But I am right there with you, my new friend. I love what you are doing."

I realized that many outreach attempts in urban areas like San Francisco are based on singing on street corners and handing out tracts. But in this case, Todd and his church were really going for it to touch these people in a very real and physical way.

Wow, how unexpected? Another surprise! Actually, I began to see the surprises as gifts. It was like God had prepared many gifts for me and put them underneath a Christmas tree to be opened one at a time. I knew they were all good since they were coming from Him, but I had not opened all of them yet.

I'll never forget the conversations with those two men, both of which are friends today. But not that long ago, I don't think I would have walked across the street to talk with either one of them. It would have been my loss for sure.

Through my former ministry involvement I certainly knew hundreds of Christians who would say they wrestled with being gay. For some reason I separated these men and women into two camps. There were those who were seeking to change and those who had accepted being gay. Until just recently I didn't realize how I had compartmentalized my view of people who are gay. Those who had accepted being gay were somehow not worth knowing, or maybe I was just afraid of crossing into the other side of all of this.

In my conversation with Todd, he invited me to attend a conference his ministry was hosting in April of 2010. I said, "Todd, I would like to come to that, but I am very low on funds and couldn't see having the money to come." He was talking about The Evangelical Network, which is an organization that has a heart to connect Christians who are gay and to support their faith and ministry efforts. Not having enough money was a great excuse to not have to think about going. I really felt quite hesitant to the thought of being at a gay-affirming conference. I had no idea what I would see there or experience.

I went to a friend's house whose name is Mike. I wanted to ask him to consider being a board member for Grace Rivers Ministry. In our conversation he was very direct with me. He was asking me to describe the focus of the ministry. I struggled to find the words that would effectively tell him what we were about. It was obviously a struggle for me to begin with. I did everything I could do to avoid homosexual or gay community. I wasn't willing to step out onto that limb and admit what was really in my heart.

Mike said something that really challenged me. "John, what is your strength? What is at the core of your heart for people and for ministry?" He went on to tell me what he saw. He emphasized my history and what he had seen in my life for many years. "John, isn't your real burden for the gay community?"

Well, I had tried to stuff that away for almost two years. But, I couldn't deny my heart. When I had only been a Christian for a year or so, I wept for those in the gay community who needed a purpose for life, a hope for the future. I asked the Lord to give me the calling to help, to share the hope that was in my own life. My heart's desire is truly for the gay community to know how much God loves them.

I couldn't deny what Mike was trying to point out. I still wanted to push it away. I wasn't sure I wanted to go back into the battle zone that often centers around homosexuality and the church. I had lived in that battle for so long I kind of liked the more generic form of ministry. It seemed to be easier to talk about and was more comfortable for many people to accept.

But Mike clarified for me that it is hard to share such a generic vision for ministry and to get people on board to walk alongside me if I didn't have a focus to tell them about. Oh, yes, generic ministry will always be a part of our lives as Christians, but it is important for me to know what my special calling really is.

Mike was right. I still had a deep burden, and it was definitely focused on people within the gay community. Meeting Michael Bussee and Todd Ferrell challenged me to a very deep place. I realized that there is an entirely different side to homosexuality that I had never explored before. I never wanted to admit that there were gay people who had a sincere heart for God who truly wanted Him to fill their lives and to follow Him to the best of their ability. Todd told me about how their church members go into the gay bars and make themselves available just to talk, to listen, and to pray for those they come into contact with.

"What? Do you mean they want to reach the gay community with Christ just like I do?"

Again, I was surprised and at the same time challenged. I recognized that I had not met many Christians who would go to those lengths to share the love of Christ with people in the gay community. Here they were, people I had judged to be rebellious and compromising, doing the very things that God called us all to do.

God had a plan for me that I had never expected. A large gift was waiting for me to open. The surprise inside was unsettling, but at the same time touched my heart deeply and brought my faith to a new place. The conflict in my own heart was about ready to begin.

The World According to a Blogger!

September 2008

I saw that there was a ministry forming that was deep in my heart. I knew it had something to do with the series I had taught as well as the new revelation of grace that was growing inside of me. Tributaries of Grace was the theme, but the name was hard to say quickly, and so I did a search for something close. I came up with Grace Rivers.

In just a couple of months, I had an official ministry name, a website, and a non-profit organization. So now we had to figure out what this was all about. I began blogging about my transition, the changes in my heart, and decided to write articles on the series I had taught. I knew there was something significant to tell others, and I had to figure out how to do it.

An old acquaintance, Todd Posey, called me to ask me some questions about a group model I had used when I was at Love In Action. He said he was coming to town so we decided to meet and discuss what was going on in our lives. When we met, he was shocked and amazed at what I was talking about and affirmed that there was a purpose and a plan in God's heart for my new vocational interests.

This meeting turned into more, and a plan was laid out! We developed a plot for what was called A Journey of Grace, and I began to write a chapter each week to process through the nine core principles that could lead someone to the same grace I had found for myself. After many weeks I had compiled a lengthy collection of topics, and Todd thought it might be a great conference format.

So a couple of months later we had another series of meetings and came up with a plan for how this material could be brought to Christian gatherings. We started marketing the conference and building a frame-work to release it. A decision was made to premier A Journey of Grace at Todd's church in Kentucky. We bought radio spots, Todd talked it up everywhere he could, and I sent out mailings to those within driving distance that were on my mailing list.

The date came and my wife and I traveled to northern Kentucky with great expectations of how this material would be received. We got ready for the Friday night event, assembled conference manuals, and waited patiently for the start time to come.

Two hours later, our seats were empty and literally NO ONE came to register. We looked at each other and said, "Well, we are going to present a conference, so here we go. I delivered each message pas-sionately to two people—my wife and Todd. Well, to be honest, Todd's pastor came to some of the sessions, so there were three people at times. But the material was presented, and recorded, without a hitch.

I certainly had to process the reality of hosting a conference out of town and no one showing up. The way I got through it was to realize it had to be God's plan because if one person would have come, it would have been worse. We figured God wanted to give us a practice run, and I really was OK with what happened and wasn't devastated. Well, I was disappointed and a little embarrassed when my friends asked me how it went. But I somehow had the confidence that God was with me through the experience. Just like in my office that day, God wasn't surprised and would work this into something good.

I came home and just kept moving forward with what was in front of me. I pondered what I might do next and what else I could write about. Todd had encouraged me to write a devotional series on the pictures that show up on the Grace Rivers website. I began with one picture and wrote what came to my heart when I originally saw the photos and picked them to represent Grace Rivers Ministry. I felt encouraged as I wrote. These articles were from my heart and were written with real people in mind who were facing real life situations.

During this first year away from over twenty years of ex-gay ministry, I kept pushing ministry to the subject of homosexuality out of my way. I kept thinking, "God, I want something radical. I don't want to contrive any ministry focus out of my past, but want to be open to Your future."

I kept looking for surprises, and they came regularly in the adjustments to a brand-new life, vocation, and career!

John Smid - A Car Salesman

August 2009

How did I end up selling cars? A while back as I was praying about how God might be able to provide a living wage for my family, I was reading a magazine that showed an ad for a new car called the SmartForTwo. The ad mentioned a dealership in Memphis, so I opened my eyes to the possibility of selling Smart Cars because of their unique design and market. I thought surely this might be an open door to an unseasoned sales person.

The next week I got ready to apply for a job and went to the Mercedes dealership where they said they were sold. When I got to the desk, I mentioned why I was there. The man standing by the desk returned my comment with a strong response, "NO, we don't sell Smart Cars. WE TURNED down that dealership. I wasn't sure how I had offended him by my comment, but there was something under the rug in his world for sure.

As I was driving away, I asked God why in the world He led me there as I knew He did. My own thoughts wondered if it were just a test of obedience. I felt relieved because I really didn't want to work there any-way. While I was out though, I went to two Starbucks coffee shops and submitted applications. They seemed more to fit my schedule and need for benefits.

A couple of weeks later I heard an advertisement for sales help at a local Toyota Dealership on our local country music station. I felt strongly that I was to go and apply for a job there. Maybe God had prepared me earlier in my heart by sending me to the Mercedes dealership.

Since I didn't have a resume, I quickly prepared one and got dressed in respectable clothing and went to the dealership. I handed my resume to the lady at the desk, and she asked me to fill out an application. She said I would likely have an interview right away.

I was introduced to the General Sales Manager who was kind and affirming of me and of my skills. He assured me I would do well at this job. He handed me off to the Sales Manager who likewise was very affirming and said that because of my history I would likely be in management in a short time. He said that he wanted me to interview with the General Manager of the dealership, so off I went to another office. His first question was, "John, do you like to read?" He recommended that I read a book on leadership called Built to Serve. He thought I would enjoy reading it and after a few other affirming words sent me on my way.

Many times I had gone over in my head my insecurities about applying for a secular job. After twenty-two years in ministry with a sexual recovery program and having never gone to college, I certainly didn't have the cutting edge for getting a good job! I couldn't imagine why someone would hire me. But in these three interviews, each person mentioned my resume and my job experience with positive reactions. They actually said that these tools showed them that I was exactly what they were looking for. One man said, "John, if you can work with sexual recovery, you can surely sell cars!" It was apparent that God was in fact opening up the door for me, so I continued walking through it. I had no idea what would happen next.

That fateful day, I was offered a job selling cars virtually on a silver platter. I returned in two days to accept the offer, and a week later I began my training. I moved through several courses in Toyota University and asked a lot of questions of the others I encountered. I also heard a lot of comments about life as a car salesman. Most mentioned the dog eat dog world and the long hours spent at work.

Along the way my energy towards this job waned. Each person in his own way told me of how he had to often console his wife because of the time away from home. They spoke often of how some people were honest, but others would go out of their way to get the next sale even it meant running over someone else to get there. Well, this is what I expected so I wasn't surprised— just shocked that I was moving into something that felt as if I were being swallowed by a beast!

A bright spot during my training was when the sales manager told me to go get the keys to the cars and drive them! You mean I can drive any car I want to? I was in seventh heaven that day, driving numerous cars to my heart's content.

When I was released to sell cars the second week, I felt comfortable and enthusiastic about this part of the job. I loved people and enjoyed cars. It seemed to be a good combination. I mean, if you have to go to work, it might just as well be something you are familiar with; and this seemed to fit the bill. My first and second customers were really enjoyable. I took some test drives with them, and it seemed I was catching them with my knowledge and my intuitive ideas.

After a couple of days, my sense was correct; I was being swallowed up by a beast all right. I was drowning in the belly of a whale and didn't know how to get out. I felt trapped by the job and drained of my heart. I had nowhere to turn but to the Lord. As I have prayed many times in my life, "God get me out of this!"

> Jonah 1:17; 2:1-10 - But the LORD provided a great fish to swallow Jonah, and Jonah was inside the fish three days and three nights.

From inside the fish Jonah prayed to the LORD his God. He said: "In my distress I called to the LORD", and he answered me. From the depths of the grave I called for help, and you listened to my cry.

You hurled me into the deep, into the very heart of the seas, and the currents swirled about me; all your waves and breakers swept over me.

I said, 'I have been banished from your sight; yet I will look again toward your holy temple.'

The engulfing waters threatened me, the deep surrounded me; seaweed was wrapped around my head.

To the roots of the mountains I sank down; the earth beneath barred me in forever. But you brought my life up from the pit, O LORD my God.

"When my life was ebbing away, I remembered you, LORD, and my prayer rose to you, to your holy temple."

Those who cling to worthless idols forfeit the grace that could be theirs.

But I, with a song of thanksgiving, will sacrifice to you. What I have vowed I will make good. Salvation comes from the LORD.

And the LORD commanded the fish, and it vomited Jonah onto dry land.

I can relate to Jonah. I had been in the belly of the whale. That week had been one of the most challenging weeks I had faced in a very long time. Monday, my first day greeting customers with the intent of selling a car, started out with pretty good energy. By Tuesday I was experiencing a change of heart. Discouragement and grief replaced my energy for the job I had taken. I began to seek the Lord while I was mowing my lawn. I poured my heart out to Him, but through the week of confusion, God hammered my heart. "What do you want, John? You can't have it both ways." I had also been hammering God's heart, " You know where my heart is at God. How much freedom do I have to pursue my heart's desire?"

The grief I was feeling went beyond what I had felt in a long time. As my wife and I were praying that morning, I said, "I sense that I am losing everything that is important to me". Because of the heavy schedule and overwhelming commitment of this new job, I had lost significant family time. I had lost contact with relationships that had become a strong support system for me. And not insignificantly, I was losing the mission the Lord had laid on my heart. It had become severely challenged because of a lack of time and focus to put into it. I had experienced a significant number of hours each day, standing on the sidewalk in front of the building, praying, and waiting for a buying customer. I felt trapped by the expectations and the reality of this kind of job. I felt lost in a world far away from my life's calling and my heart's desire.

When I entered the job at the car dealership, I did so quickly and had clouded eyes, thinking that God was calling me to this to meet our financial needs and that He might have something in this for me that is important for my walk with Him and for Grace Rivers. As I faced each day, I had a different conversation with the Lord and actually I found that He was speaking to me in a fatherly way that I appreciated.

I had to evaluate who I am at the core of my being. How did God create me and what is His calling on my life? I had no question about how I would answer that. Standing in front of the sales lot was certainly neither energizing nor fulfilling. I questioned whether or not I was just in an adjustment period and needed to stick with this since I started it. But my experience led to a deeper evaluation.

As I honestly looked down the road, I could see that being at this job longer would not make things better. I had already made some friends, and I knew that would help in this becoming more fulfilling. But as I honestly looked at the bigger picture, I could see that the longer I was there, the further away from my heart I would be. I had to ask myself if I were willing to lose more of my heart and if God were actually saying He was changing my calling.

This is why I was feeling grieved— I was losing something. All that I had built up over the last year could be lost if I didn't get my butt up and accept the challenge that God had placed before me. He was asking me if I were willing to put the same energy into Grace Rivers that I would have had to put into selling cars. I did not believe in my heart of hearts that God had placed me on this earth to sell cars. I would know that if it were true. He does give us the desires of our heart - He shows us what they are! I also have a responsibility now to engage my body and energy into that desire.

While I was in training, another salesman asked me what I had learned in my two weeks there. I didn't have a full answer for him at the time, but I believe God was truly speaking through my friend. I learned how to step into this job that was clearly an open door, trusting God would lead me where He wanted me to go. I learned that there is potentially a kingdom value in everything we do. I learned that I can make a left turn going a different direction and how to trust God in that decision. I also learned that when I get a little way down the road, I could make a u-turn and go back. I also learned that during that detour, God was present, available, and would take full advantage of the experience. I learned more about seeking God for my heart's desire.

I now consider myself back on track but differently from before. I am motivated in a new way to seek something with all my heart. I am more trustful right now of God's direction and of His plans for me. I also realize that I have some work to do.

I am more willing to be honest with myself, my wife, others, and, not the least, more honest with God. I am learning more about authenticity. How God has wired me maybe? Sorry, the word "authenticity" again. And learning more about transparency for sure.

A friend of mine and I talked of how we could minister to others through personal meetings designed to read the Bible together, listen to each other, and encourage each other toward a mission-oriented life. So I reached out to a group of men to see if they might want to meet with me one on one. I set a goal of inviting six men into this arrangement. Within a week, not only had six responded, but I had filled my schedule with ten men whom I began to meet with regularly.

I loved the meetings and began to discover a new-found heart within me as I sought to be a source of encouragement for them. I spent time discovering what I saw that was good in each of their lives. As we met, I prayed for God to show me how I could encourage them.

Those who know me would say that this was not exactly what I was doing in the previous years of ministry. I was used to looking for the shortcomings, the loose ends of someone's life. I had a sense of pride in my ability to challenge people with those things that needed to be corrected. So, this ministry approach was significantly new for me. My journey continues.

I Found Grace

July 2009

As the second year of my departure from Love In Action came along, I was feeling satisfied, I was challenged in areas of my heart that were brand new for me to look at. I was also finding a much needed rest in my soul, and Jesus was coming into these new areas that had opened up.

I was gaining a new understanding of an old word, grace. What is grace and how does this apply to our Christian walk? I wasn't sure I truly understood it from personal experience. I had always heard, "Grace is the unmerited favor of God upon our lives."

One day when I was sitting in my office alone, I wandered into something I had never experienced before. I thought to myself, Hmm, I don't work for Love In Action any more. I've never chosen to look at anything pornographic on the internet. I wonder what is actually out there.

So, within a few clicks of the mouse I found some pictures that drew my interest. I looked a little more; then all of a sudden my heart SANK! "Oh, my God, what have I done? I just crossed over the bridge into forbidden land. I have broken a place in my life that I have never strayed into before—NEVER!"

My mind began to rush into all of the years of instruction, of challenges for others, and into fears of "What do I do now?" My mind was scrambling, and anxiety filled my heart. Then all of a sudden, something came to me that would become a life-changing, life-transforming experience with Jesus.

"John, what is the deepest thing you know about Me?" Jesus spoke through my anxious heart. I replied, "There is therefore now no condemnation for those who are in Christ Jesus." He said, "Apply that right now." I began a whole new process of prayer with Jesus. I began to unravel the last few minutes as I have never done before. "Lord, You have not condemned me, so I will not receive any condemnation from You for what I have chosen to do."

Then the Lord said, "John, why are you here? What has brought you to look at those pictures?" I began a dialogue with Him about all of that, realizing that a lot of it was motivated by my own curiosity. After pondering the questions that brought me to search the internet, I heard Jesus say: "John, do you have any more questions?" In my own amazement with this conversation I said, "No, no I don't think so." Then He said, "Well, then, I guess we are done with this for now, aren't we."

Oh—I just experienced something about grace that I have never experienced before in my entire life! At a point where I felt as though I had just committed the unpardonable sin, Jesus came into my heart with such calmness. He didn't yell, He didn't shame me, He didn't scold me or embarrass me. He just acknowledged me, listened to my heart, and in many ways, brought me into a teaching moment with Him right there.

I realized, duh! That Jesus was beside me the whole time. This wasn't a surprise to Him. But even more, He also put all of this into perspective. It wasn't so much about the pictures I ventured into. He seemed to be far more interested in our relationship. That was far more important to Him than the clicking of my mouse while I looked to satisfy my own curiosity.

God became man, right inside my own heart, and dwelt with me! He showed me a personal side of our relationship that was one of the most significant experiences with Him I have ever had! He revealed to me just how close He is and how much He loves me.

I found a new revelation of the life-transforming power of grace. I learned something about humankind that had never crossed my mind before. All of the challenges, confrontations, preaching the truth I had done in the past didn't hold a candle to meeting with Jesus and finding His love and incredible ability to show me the truth that there is no condemnation from His heart to mine, if I am in Him.

As I pondered His message of grace to my heart, something quite dramatic began to change in the way I handled every relationship I encountered. I began to process life challenges so differently with all of this in mind. I saw life as a journey rather than a performance test. I filtered what I previously called sinful behavior with grace in mind. Grace that is forgiveness, transformation, God's covering and His incredible way of turning everything around in our lives to something that is good. In just small ways I saw how I had lived a life of shame and how I place this shame onto others along the way. Now I had something tangible to use as a tool of evaluation of the ministry in which I had been so deeply involved.

A Formal Apology

March 2010

For many years I have contemplated the times I have heard that some people have said they were harmed or wounded from their experience with Love In Action or Exodus International. More often than not my reactions have not been favorable. In my own mind I didn't feel there was any merit to the accusations. After all, I have given 22 years of my life sacrificially just to hear how we harmed you!

Well I certainly know the sound of a defensive reaction when I hear one! I was it! I didn't want to hear anything that was critical or negative. But, I believe in listening to the heart of others no matter how critical it may sound. I needed to check in on my own heart to see if there was any validation to their comments. Of course, there was.

Since I was in leadership with both organizations I have certainly been at the center of many of the criticisms. The scripture challenges us to be careful with what we say and do as leaders because of the higher standard that is expected and deserved from those whom we care for.

In the last two years I have had a lot of time to ponder, pray, and sort through many facets of my vocational ministry history. Since I have had a lot of alone time my searching has been easier to handle.

As I continue to transition away from having worked with ex-gay ministry for many years, an editor from a well read blog called the Ex-gay Watch contacted me about my resignation from Love In Action. He began to ask me questions about why I had chosen to leave and what was going on in my life at the time. As we talked, I shared with him about how my heart had become more open to building relationships within the gay community. He recommend that I come up with an apology first. He talked with me about how many people within the gay community didn't trust the ex-gay community and that if I could find it in my heart to apologize for things I had done to wound them through my involvement with Love In Action, it might help me to build a trust in order to be heard.

I wasn't sure I was ready for that. I didn't know what an apology would consist of and how my life had wounded others. But, my mind was open because I wanted to badly to develop this outreach to bring the gospel into the lives of those that were gay. The request for an apology became deeply lodged into my heart, and I began to pray about what that may entail. God brought some things into my life to help me see what that may look like.

As I prepared a draft of what I thought an apology would look like I took it to a meeting I had with Morgan Fox. I asked him for his input. Surprisingly, he came back with some really good and challenging insights.

He talked with me about some of what I had written that sounded to him like I was making excuses, or rationalizing some of the things I had done. He was right! For many years I thought if I could explain my reasoning then the other person would understand and somewhere in the conversation there would be a release of the conflict.

In this case, I took Morgan's advice and worked as hard as I knew how to just state the facts and not give any background reasons or excuses. I was really appreciative of Morgan's willingness to help and many might be surprised to know he was involved in writing the apology.

From John J. Smid to the readers of Ex-gay Watch

Just a little bit of history here. I became a Christian in 1982. My new faith created conflicts in my homosexual relationship and eventually I ended the relationship I was in. It was at that point I decided to pursue my relationship with Jesus instead of looking for a new relationship right away.

When I had been celibate for several years I felt that I wanted to be married to a woman. I had been married previously and in my heart wanted to give that a try again.

I met my wife Vileen in 1985 and we married in 1988. We have had a good, faithful marriage just as I had hoped. I told her about my homosexuality right after we had met. She has walked alongside me knowing that I have chosen her rather than to pursue a homosexual relationship. She is aware that my attractions haven't changed in general towards men but that I love her deeply and make choices daily to remain faithful to our marriage and have not regretted that decision.

In 1986 I moved to San Rafael California to work as a volunteer for Love In Action. I am passionate about people and spent 22 years with Love In Action. Since Exodus International was in our same office most of those years I also became involved with them right away.

By 1995 I had been involved in Love In Action and Exodus for nine years and was asked to give a talk in a general session at the Exodus national conference. God had brought me to a point where I was willing to admit to myself that I still had homosexual attractions. As a result of my own internal process of disclosure I decided to give my talk on the topic of honesty. I spoke of my current homosexual attractions and challenged the audience to be honest with themselves. I have always been as intentional as I could to share freely about those things whenever I speak or meet with someone who can relate to homosexuality.

On June 6th of 2005, when the protestors showed up on the sidewalks in front of Love In Action to speak against the Refuge Program, my world was rocked. But within just a couple of days my heart was humbled by the gracious words coming from those who were outside such as God Loves You. The truth spoken from them caused me to think and began to soften my heart.

A lot has changed since then. God does love me and He loved me enough to continue to shave off some things in my life that have been wrong, offensive, calloused and judgmental. Through the humility of Morgan Fox, one of the leaders of the protest, I was humbled once again. His pursuit of a relationship with me, though I did not deserve it, has been another tool that God has used to break through parts of my heart that needed to be touched.

Morgan asked me to interview for a documentary he is producing about the protests. I resisted for a long time. After many meetings with Morgan I began to see his godly character and agreed to an interview because I trusted him. During our camera time the discussions involved things from the past that have been said about Love In Action or about me as the former leader. I had spent many hours and in some cases years, pondering these things and wondered how I could make amends for the things that had hurt or wounded others during my 22 years of leadership with Love In Action. Certainly there were many.

In 1994 an article was written that said that I told a young man it would be better for him to commit suicide than for him to go into the gay lifestyle. I have been haunted by that article all through the years. I have felt defensive, reactionary and frustrated every time I have read it not knowing how I could in any way, clear it away. Maybe this will help.

I want to publicly say to the young man, "I am very sorry for the conversation that I had with you that fateful day. I loved you very much as a brother and feel deeply grieved for the way that my words hurt you." If I could, I would erase the conversation and start all over with "I love you, and as you move on I will pray for God's very best for you in your life. No matter what you do, Jesus deeply loves you. Please forgive me."

Some people have spoken out about being wounded through their experience with Love In Action. " I want to say I am very sorry for the things that have wounded you or hurt you by my hands of leadership at Love In Action or anything I have done personally that has harmed you." "Please forgive me."

I was a member of the board of directors of Exodus International for eleven years. I spoke on many occasions in general sessions and in workshops at the national conferences for most of the 22 years I was involved in Love In Action and Exodus. Thousands of men and women came to Exodus ministries and conferences looking for a hand, seeking hope, or for someone to hear their heart and understand.

I am a very verbal person and can speak at times without thoroughly thinking through what I might say before it comes out of my mouth. Without question I know I have said things that may have hurt someone or caused confusion or discouragement. Please forgive me for the things I have said that were not helpful or were further damaging of your tender heart.

As a board member of Exodus International I felt a strong sense of stewardship for the lives we hoped we would impact with the love of Jesus. I have learned a lot more over the last couple of years about how unconditional His love really is. I believe I could have done a better job of letting people know that Jesus loves them purely because He does, unconditionally. I am sorry for not being a better vessel of the Love of Christ to those who deeply need to know of His love. I realize I was often more concerned with telling people how to live than I was with imparting God's grace so that they would want to live!

Now, regarding the most highly publicized Refuge Program for teens that was held through Love In Action. If I could go back and do anything differently based on what I know today – it would be the Refuge Program. I have a hard time admitting it but the protests did bring about a season for me to reevaluate my life, my heart, and the Refuge Program. God did an amazing work in me through the challenges that resulted from the people who came to the streets in front of our ministry, morning and night, for two weeks.

I really wanted to help the young men in our program but in some cases the design of our program caused more harm for some of these kids that it did good. I am very sorry for the ways that Refuge further wounded teens that were already in a very delicate place in life. I am grateful for the way that God lovingly called us to revamp the methods for dealing with families with teens so that more teens weren't hurt.

I have been a Christian for almost 30 years. There are myriads of things that I do or that go through my mind that aren't biblically appropriate. There are many things that God wants me to change in my own life so that I can be a better person; love Him more and love others better. I do not want a judgmental heart to separate me from people that I love dearly.

It has been almost two years since I left the ministry of Love In Action in May of 2008. I have had many days and hours alone to think and ponder the last 22 years. God has dug deep into my heart and caused me to see something very important that he wanted me to know. He loves me unconditionally. His grace is sufficient for me. I cannot do anything that He hasn't forgiven, isn't forgiving, and won't forgive and it is up to Him to restore my soul, I can't do that myself.

I am not the judge and jury of other people. I can't see another person's heart like He can. I cannot redeem anyone, only He can. I don't know what someone might need today but he does.

If you have been wounded by me or harmed through the hands of my leadership; please come to me and allow an opportunity for me to personally apologize with the hope that we can both be released from the bondage of unforgiveness.

I am leading a new ministry called Grace Rivers. It's primary focus isn't to be an ex-gay ministry but within the context of offering grace and the Love of Jesus to our world we are starting grace groups for people impacted by homosexuality.

As a brand new start, Grace Rivers is an outpouring of the many of the changes in my own heart. I have based this work on nine core values starting with honesty, moving on to listening to others effectively, and in the end giving respect because God does. I have attempted to pursue these values in my own life to the best of my ability. God is still working on restoring me so I know He is doing the same with others. We are all on a road of life that is hopefully improving day by day. He says He will complete the work He has started so I trust Him fully with my life and with the lives of others who know Him.

Amazing Life Stories

April 2010

About a week or two after Todd Ferrell and I talked for the first time I got a call from a ministry in Washington State. It seemed they wanted me to facilitate a conference for their area that would include mostly ministry to the parents of gay children. I wanted to do it, so I said I would put it down on the calendar. As soon as I looked, I found that Todd's conference was just one weekend after I had scheduled to be in Washington.

How interesting? I talked with my wife and realized I could easily arrange a circle trip to accommodate a flight from Washington to Southern California that would only slightly change my airfare. I called Todd and said I could now come to the conference he was holding. I was extremely nervous about attending this conference with Christians that are gay. Years ago I learned not to criticize something that I was unfamiliar with so for no other reason than to look and see for myself, I felt I needed to attend the event.

As time came closer I asked Todd about a referral for a hotel roommate. I just didn't have the money to front the entire cost and was looking for someone to share that with me. Of course, I was trusting in Todd to find someone appropriate and knew he would understand my situation. So as the weeks went by, Todd contacted me with the name of a good friend of his that he said would have a lot in common with me. His name was Gary.

So, I completed the conference in Washington and flew to Los Angeles. I had arranged to stay with some good friends there for a couple of days just prior to Todd's conference. I spent a lot of time talking with them about my plans and running this decision through our friendship filter.

I was very anxious the morning of April 29, 2010, as my friend drove me to the front door of the hotel and dropped me off. I felt extremely self-conscious going into the hotel. My mind was racing with questions and fears. Once I was inside, I got registered and went to my room. Gary, my roommate, was already there, so I introduced myself to him. He was very gracious, and we decided to have a meal together that evening and get to know each other. I found him to be a wonderful guy. He was about my age.

He had previously been married and had a daughter. His marriage had ended in divorce, but they had done a lot of work to become amicable and had become good friends as they raised their daughter. He was kind, and honest as he shared his story. And, he was gracious with my story as well.

The next morning I went to the first workshop and walked inside and saw someone that looked very familiar to me. As the morning went by, I knew for certain it was the man I remembered. I really wanted to talk with him. As we walked out the door I turned to him and said, "Hello, do you know where we know each other from?" He looked puzzled and then I told him. "You were in the Love In Action program in the mid-eighties. I was there as a House Leader and remember you very well." He laughed and embraced me and then seemed really glad to see me. He was using a walker which at his age told me he was going through something difficult. I was so glad to see him. His smile was so joyous and he seemed to be so in love with Jesus which showed through every pore in his body.

He began to tell me about the last 20 years of his life. He was HIV +, he had just had surgery for cancer and was in recovery, hence, the walker. He said he had lost many friends through his recent illness, and he said that today his family was all he had. And yet through all of the pain and suffering, he said, "But I love Jesus. He has been so good to me." He went on to say that he was really glad he had been in Love In Action because it was where he learned how much he needed the Lord. He talked very easily about how messed up his life was when he went there and that the experience at Love In Action helped him to begin his own journey of healing and growing in Christ. "John, I'm gay and I'm OK with that. Jesus loves me and I've never been so complete and satisfied in Him." There were several people that I met that weekend that really challenged me to listen to them without judgment.

I was so surprised! I never expected the first person I would see, other than my friendly roommate, to be one of the first people I met when I began working with Love In Action so many years ago. He and I talked often over the next several days of the conference and every time I saw him, he was encouraging someone, laughing with someone or showing evidence of a wonderful connection to the Lord. There is nowhere else he would have gotten that kind of joy.

I tried to remain as invisible as I could so, I began to listen to others and closely evaluate what I was seeing and hearing. On the evening of that first day I decided to go to the common area to relax. When I got there, I saw two younger guys who were talking with each other. I introduced myself to them. They asked if I were part of the conference. I hesitated to affirm their question but said, "yes". They said "Oh, that's wonderful, so are we." Just a few short surface questions later they asked if they could share their story with me. I obliged their seeming hunger to tell me more about their life experiences.

Once again, I was shocked at what I heard. "John, we were huge druggies. We have known each other from the drug culture for over fifteen years. We've been together since we were teenagers." They went on to talk about how their pastor pursued them for over four years. "John, his kindness and his faithfulness finally won out. We accepted Christ a year ago. It has been an amazing journey for us. We have seen a real change for the better in our lives and in our relationship with each other." It was apparent to me they were talking about their same sex partnership for fifteen years or more now.

I'm sure if someone had looked at me they might have seen my head spinning in disbelief of what I was experiencing. I had such a deep hunger to see people come to know Jesus in a real, solid, life changing way. Right here before my eyes was the answer to my prayers. But it didn't look as I had thought it would. These young men were obviously very excited about Jesus and truly understood the gospel. Yet they were seemingly very comfortable in their relationship and with being gay.

From their relationship with Jesus, their lives were changing for sure, but not in ways I would have expected. I had always assumed that an acceptance of Christ would have brought a increasing discomfort of a gay relationship in two guys who were seeking Him like these two guys were. They told me how much of a mess it has been for their pastor to walk alongside of them, yet he had continued to love them. One of the guys said, "My parents didn't used to like my partner when we were drugging. But now, they say they are thrilled because of the positive influence he has had on me in my growth in God and how he has encouraged my faith."

Then, they talked about how they wanted to go to the beach while they were in Southern California, but decided not to. I asked why not? And their answer was another example of their walk with Christ. I saw the fruit in their next statement, "Oh, we don't think it would be a good idea; we're trying to keep our minds pure and seeing all the guys on the beach might not be helpful."

As I spun around in my head from what I had just experienced, I got up and said goodbye. I went up to my room and just felt such a sense of joy for God allowing me to hear the real life story of these two guys. But at the same time, their story challenged so much of my own doctrine that I was unsettled and questioning so many things.

When I got back to my room, Gary was still up. We talked late into the night. He shared a lot of his own life with me, and I told him most of mine. We really connected. I loved his sensitivity to my life, and his own humility was amazing for me to experience. He was genuine in his faith yet was comfortable in being gay. He seemed to have found a place where both resided in his life with peace. All of this challenged my former philosophies. I had always said that God would not allow anyone who is His to find peace if they had embraced being gay. I just assumed that God would certainly cause them to be unsettled, convicted, or at odds with Him and themselves at a deep level.

This process for me has been interesting, threatening, and life shaking. This was just the first day of this conference. The next two days weren't any less earth shattering for me. I remained on the periphery of the groups and just kept a low profile.

As I continue to experience the three day conference, more stories come to my mind of God's abundant grace and how He has impacted so many people who were there.

I experienced another curious meeting as I was standing in the lobby of the hotel, where the conference was being held, I saw my two new friends from last night. As I walked up to them they were talking with an older man and introduced me, "John, this is our pastor, the one who has accepted the challenge of discipling us." I entered the conversation with them for a few minutes and the two guys excused themselves. A lady was standing with us and I was introduced to Rene.

Rene was someone I noticed in all of the main sessions. She seemed to always stand on the periphery of the room. She was very tall and from my observation seemed to be a transsexual. As the pastor introduced us he began to talk about Rene. He told me that his church had tried an outreach ministry to the transsexual community around them but had not had much success. He continued to share with me that transsexuals are often emotionally immature and challenging due to their emotional development of eight or nine years of age.

I turned to Rene and said, "How do you feel about this discussion about you taking place?" Rene took off and ran with her story. She said she agreed about the emotional immaturity issues. She then said, "John, transsexuals don't often want to be on center stage. It is a challenge for me to get this attention." Then, what she said next was astonishing to hear!

"I consider my life in Christ to be like that of a warhorse. A warhorse is trained to obey its master completely, even if the rider takes it into a brick wall. I see my walk with God like that. It's uncomfortable to be talked about or to be brought into the front line of a conversation. But, my pastor asked me to start a fellowship for transsexuals. I knew the need was there, wasn't comfortable taking that kind of leadership role, but I wanted to be obedient to the calling. So, I began the group on Sunday afternoons."

The pastor then stepped in and affirmed that the group was going well and that the ministry he wasn't able to get off the ground, was working underneath the leadership of Rene's shepherding heart and care for these people. We talked a little bit more and then went to our next session.

I was completely shocked and amazed at what I had just heard. In my former association with ex-gay ministry, I would have quickly assessed this as completely wrong for Rene to be living as she is, doing what she is doing, and following God into what she believed He had led her into. We would have questioned her motives, challenged her clothing, and certainly would have never found her qualified for any Christian ministry leadership.

But this day was different for me. I had laid my opinions aside for this conference. I wanted to take a neutral position so that I could hear the stories, experience the atmosphere, and hopefully listen to God's heart. I could not deny that Rene loved God, loved others, and desired more than anything to serve the Savior with her very being. She wasn't a renegade, or rebellious. Quite the contrary, she was living a self sacrificial life for the good of others.

As I walked away I found myself saying "Who else is willing, who else could God find that would love these people?" This experience certainly blew more of my preconceived ideas about someone being holy enough to find a place in the service of our Lord. I have often said, "If God can't use imperfect people, He can't use any of us". However, my introduction to Rene took my own words to a deeper place of reality. I am incredibly thankful for Rene, her heart, her sacrifice, and her dedication to give back to Jesus from a thankful heart of what He has already given her.

I kept processing my experience with my roommate Gary. He was a great listener and quite gracious with my wordy processing of the weekend. He listened intently and would often share his own reflections with me.

On Saturday they had a panel of what was called straight allies. I had never heard that term before but I knew that the presence of these four men at this event was huge, groundbreaking and, in many ways, unprecedented. One has to consider that, just their mere appearance at this type of event could be a big risk for them, as there's just not that many that call themselves straight allies in the Christian community right now. But, maybe even more significant, these men chose to, not only attend this conference but also chose to be an integral part by participating in this panel.

The men who participated were Chuck Smith Jr. (son of Chuck Smith Sr, the father of the Jesus Movement and the founder of the huge network of Calvary Chapel churches around the globe) who was on the end. Sitting next to Chuck Smith Jr was Andrew Marin (author of Love is An Orientation).

Then there was Jay Bakker (son of Jim and Tammy Faye Bakker). And, next to Jay was Mark Tidd (Evangelical pastor of Denver's The Highland's Church). As the panel talked, each one shared his stories of meeting men and women in the gay community who loved God and wanted to serve Him. They shared how meeting these gay folks had challenged their own theologies regarding the gay issue, their historical views of homosexuality, and how they had seen the scriptures differently since they began to look into themselves in light of what they were experiencing.

I really related to these men. When I moved away from twenty two years of conservative ex-gay ministry and got alone with God myself, it seemed He was shaking loose some of the things I had always thought and had been taught. I was challenged by these men on the panel and their seeming care and love for the people here at this conference.

I could sense that some people here were avoiding contact with me. Todd had warned me that I would not be well received here by some of those in attendance. I think he was right. But at the same time, others lovingly accepted my presence.

One afternoon, a man walked in whom I had previously only met on the phone. Michael Bussee introduced himself to me. Michael was one of the co-founders of Exodus International, the world's largest ex-gay organization. (Michael is now a very outspoken advocate for the gay-affirming community). We immediately embraced each other with a warm hug. We decided to find a quiet place where we could talk. When we sat down in the designated prayer room. It was as if we had known each other for many, many years. We talked, shared, and seemed to understand each other. We were interrupted by a conference worker who informed us that this room had a designated purpose and that we should find another place to talk. I didn't want our conversation to end. I was really enjoying our conversation and connection. Michael didn't have a lot of time. He had other engagements he was committed to, so we said our goodbyes.

Saturday there was a meeting of the leaders and affiliate organizations which Todd graciously invited me to attend. Each one gave a report of the year of ministry. As I listened, I heard one after the other share about the opportunities they had to reach out with the gospel of Jesus Christ. One stood out to me because of something that caused my mind to do some shifting. This lady talked about how thankful they were to have their church gathering in the local gay community center. At first I thought "of course, they are gay." But then I realized they were excited because of the opportunity to reach into the local gay community with a message of salvation and hope.

One workshop that lasted six hours impacted me greatly. It was taught by Joseph Pearson, an older man who was highly intelligent, well studied, and passionate about his message. He was teaching on what he saw in the scriptures concerning the subject of homosexuality. I am not going into the teachings or my specific reaction in this writing, but will save that for another time. I will say this. In twenty five years, I have been unwilling to even read anything that was contrary to my understanding of what the scriptures said about homosexuality. What's to question? In my mind when I went into this workshop, homosexuality is sin and that's it. I believed the bible to be very clear and absolutely unquestionable on this subject.

When the workshop was finished, I was willing to accept that there is a great controversy over this issue. Men who are learned, intelligent, well studied on Scripture and well educated on culture, context, language, and application disagree on this subject.

I certainly left with many further questions on my mind. I wasn't sorry I went to the workshop and actually, it led me to do some deeper study myself upon my return home.

Afterwards I talked with Joseph personally. He told me of his relationship with his partner of thirty years. He said, "John, many times we encountered difficulties that could have caused us to separate. But in thirty years of being together, we decided to stick it out, work it through and we have been faithful to each other through all of these years." As I walked away, once again, I was very interested in what I had just heard.

As I prepared to end my time with this conference I began to do some evaluation of the entire experience. I heard people throughout the weekend that were excited about Jesus. Over and over I listened to testimonies, celebration with enthusiasm about how God was so gracious, kind, and loving. It was very clear to me that many of those attending were so close to Jesus that they were passionate about sharing Him with others. This was surprising to me. I expected something very different.

I have to admit that there have been many conferences I had attended before that were not as focused on Jesus and the gospel. I have to admit that I haven't seen this priority at many conferences I had attended through my own Christian history.

When I had entered the conference just a couple of days earlier, I expected to find a bunch of gay people who were focused on their homosexuality, and certainly not centered on Jesus. I was surprised to find there was literally no sense of seduction or sensuality from anyone that I met or experienced.

This weekend conference was centered on worship, learning, and sharing in their faith in Christ. Other than the fact there were some same sex couples there, most were single adults coming together with a common goal in their faith. That was to know Jesus more and to experience more of Him in a corporate setting.

I came home with a lot to think about. About a month later, Todd asked me to join their conference call with the affiliates. He asked me to share my observations with them from the conference. I agreed to join them, and the call occurred. At the end, he asked one lady to pray for our time together and for me.

As she prayed, I have never felt so loved, understood, and accepted by a time of prayer. Her words soaked through my skin, into the soul of my being. Afterwards I asked Todd who that was. He told me and I realized something that really impacted me.

When I was at the conference, I noticed a lady who seemed to me to be one of those people that some may not readily understand due to an outward appearance. I profiled her by her appearance. Through her prayer for me, I was deeply humbled by her sense of the Lord and ability to connect to my heart.

God has certainly surprised me again through this experience. I came away much richer from having been there, and with these people.

I Cannot Fail!

June 2010

As I pondered the message of God's grace I couldn't help but remember so many bible passages that undergirded what was going on in my heart. I began to write an article on my new revelation of God's love for me.

I think this message is one of the most important messages for us to understand as believers in Christ. As I read, and reread what I have written I get so excited within my soul that I can hardly wait to enter the day ahead of me.

This devotional isn't some plastic, great idea that I hope will encourage you. I wrote this about a year ago and I am as excited today as I was when I wrote it. I hope you will be too.

Sitting with several other men at my weekly men's bible study God brought an answer to a week of turmoil that had me in a very discouraging place. I was struggling with a sense of failure, hungry for something from the Lord that would help. Suddenly during our discussion on the Holy Spirit, God showed up! He brought the answer from a very different place than I had anticipated. From within my relationship with God He showed me an aspect of Himself that I had never seen before.

For more than a year, I had been relishing in a new found understanding of the unconditional love of Jesus. I had begun to grasp the greatness of His freedom from what the bible calls the laws of sin and death in a very personal way. I had found there was nothing I would do that will cause Jesus to love me anymore or any less than He does. This had been wonderful and transforming for me but this week something new hit me.

God is three in one, the great mystery of the trinity. I was learning about Jesus more but now, something new rose up about another facet of the Godhead! The Holy Spirit. Through the study of His word, we read through many passages that spoke of the Holy Spirit and my heart began to listen to a very personal message from Him.

> "I love you; I am your greatest encourager. I believe in you when you don't believe in yourself. I pray for you perfectly when you haven't a clue how to pray. I not only believe in you, but also plan for you that you will dis-cover over time that will amaze you! When you think you have failed, I have already begun to turn your seem-ing failure into something good and in time you will be thankful even for the greatest mistakes you have made."

> "I will empower you into growth and maturity that you can-not even imagine today. I will keep you from harm. I will order your steps. I will give courage to face things you would naturally run from. I will speak for you, in you, with you, and through you with words you didn't even know you had. I am your most passionate cheerleader and your best coach. With Me beside you, you cannot fail."

Oh, man! That was amazing to me. I can't fail? But I had felt such failure in my life. The consequences to my decisions had been great. But He reminded me that in all of my mistakes and seemingly failed decisions, He, the Holy Spirit, had brought them all around for growth, blessing, and made good come out of them that I would have never imagined!

I made the decision that this week I was going to spend a significant amount of energy pondering the amazing, God ordained, powerful impact that the Holy Spirit had on me each and every day in walking beside me, in me, and through me. I was going to focus on remembering that I have the universe's most energetic cheerleader supporting me. I also have the world's greatest coach leading, mentoring, and teaching me how to live each day. But not only is He the best cheerleader and coach, He is also the one and only transformer of my heart.

The Holy Spirit, the Comforter of my soul, the Mighty Counselor, the Omnipotent God! If He is for me, who can be against me? He is not the accuser, Satan is. He is not the one who holds it against me, condemns me, or beats me on the head! That is the enemy of my soul!

The Holy Spirit is not a wind, not a power. He is my personal trainer that always believes in me. I will not fail because of Him. God brought me an incredible answer to the cry of my heart. I can only thank Him even more for the freedom He is bringing me from condemnation and shame of this world and into His marvelous light!

I have given just a few scripture references that bring this to light. I recommend looking into others that describe the Holy Spirit's love for us and His role in our lives to do the good work of God in us. There are hundreds! He really wants us to know how much He believes in us and will not let us fail.

Ps. 42:5

Why, my soul, are you downcast?

Why so disturbed within me?

Put your hope in God, for I will yet praise him, my Savior and my God.

Ps. 56:9

Then my enemies will turn back when I call for help.

By this I will know that God is for me.

John 14:16,26

And I will ask the Father, and he will give you another advocate to help you and be with you forever—

But the Advocate, the Holy Spirit, whom the Father will send in my name, will teach you all things and will remind you of everything I have said to you.

Romans 8:1,26

Therefore, there is now no condemnation for those who are in Christ Jesus, In the same way, the Spirit helps us in our weakness. We do not know what we ought to pray for, but the Spirit himself intercedes for us through wordless groans.

Ephesians 2:4-7

But because of his great love for us, God, who is rich in mercy, made us alive with Christ even when we were dead in transgressions—it is by grace you have been saved. And God raised us up with Christ and seated us with him in the heavenly realms in Christ Jesus, in order that in the coming ages he might show the incomparable riches of his grace, expressed in his kindness to us in Christ Jesus.

Rev. 12:10

Then I heard a loud voice in heaven say:

"Now have come the salvation and the power and the kingdom of our God, and the authority of his Messiah. For the accuser of our brothers and sisters, who accuses them before our God day and night, has been hurled down."

The Bible and Homosexuality?

July 2010

As we all know, there are distinct differences in the way that people read the bible and interpret what it has to say.

I have a meeting each week with a bible mentor. I often come to him with questions about what a passage says and how we should interpret it. After my participation in the six hour workshop on the bible and homosexuality I attended at The Evangelical Network conference, I had a whole list of scriptures which, of course, was too much for one of our sessions together. I decided to begin with 1 Corinthians 6:9-11.

I walked into his office and said, "OK, I want to know. What does this really say? Can we sit down and tear this apart? Can we get to the real meaning of what Paul was actually saying here?"

> "Don't you know that the wicked will not inherit the kingdom of God? Do not be deceived: Neither the sexually immoral nor idolaters nor adulterers nor male prostitutes nor homosexual offenders nor thieves nor the greedy nor drunkards nor slanderers nor swindlers will inherit the kingdom of God. And that is what some of you were.

> But you were washed, you were sanctified, you were justified in the name of the Lord Jesus Christ and by the Spirit of our God" (1 Corinthians 6:9-11, NIV).

This passage is one that I have struggled with for over twenty years. For some, this passage has brought a lot of comfort because it speaks to one of the most exciting things about the gospel. "You were washed, you were sanctified, you were justified in the name of the Lord Jesus Christ. . . ." Anytime we see a passage that encourages us with the dramatic change that occurs when we receive the message from Jesus of a new life in Him, that is wonderful. However, this passage has also caused a lot of divisive discussion and, for many, a wrong understanding of what it says, bringing despair, hopelessness, and fear! " . . . will not inherit the kingdom of God." Do all gays go to hell? Do gossips go to hell? Do slanderers go to hell? What about the greedy; do they all go to hell too? If so, we have a huge problem.

Within the ex-gay world, verse 11—"And that is what some of you were"—speaks to a significant change in Christ. But some take this verse to mean a change in homosexual orientation. This interpretation has led to a tremendous amount of controversy through the years. What does Paul really say here about change?

There is a common misunderstanding of verse 9,"Do you not know that the wicked will not inherit the kingdom of God? "and verse 10, "…will (not) inherit the kingdom of God." This confusion has brought many people to a tremendous fear for the salvation for their own souls and for their loved ones who have admitted a struggle with homosexuality. The lack of a solid teaching on this passage has caused a tremendous amount of harm to endless numbers of people through the years. Many have taught this passage, or by omission, led people to believe that the gospel is centered on our behavior and therefore a good works oriented salvation. Paul speaks very heavily to those who lead others back to the law through many of his letters.

It is amazing that one verse can bring such a diverse reaction. From great hope to tremendous fear and despair, it has appeared to me that some, with good intentions, have greatly misunderstood the real meaning and intention in Paul's heart as he wrote these words. It became obvious to me that this verse has often not been understood, and in my own mind, I needed to study it more deeply. The impact on people's lives is at stake. I realized that further clarity was imperative.

In years past as I would try to teach on these verses, I knew that the gospel was NOT contingent on anyone's behavior. Therefore I knew that this verse could not possibly be saying that someone who was gay would not be allowed into the kingdom of God for eternity. So, my way of softening the blow (not conviction of what it actually said) was to teach that it didn't mean the eternal kingdom, but rather was just referring to the kingdom now.

Therefore, I would often try to explain that if someone described in these verses could miss out on experiencing the goodness of God's kingdom now, but it didn't mean they would be lost for eternity.

I felt settled in teaching that interpretation for many years. But I also felt conflicted because I was not confident that is what it was saying. I just didn't have any other answers.

As my bible friend and I began to review this passage, my understanding grew tremendously on why I was so unsettled about my previous teaching. My convictions were right. My mind had not grasped the real concept Paul was trying to convey. I asked some key questions:

Whom is Paul speaking to?

What was the surrounding culture at the time and how did it relate to Paul's letter?

What is the larger story of this passage?

As my friend and I dug into the Greek language, the culture, and the overall story, I was amazed! Suddenly, these verses became abundantly clear. I was encouraged, hopeful, and passionate about what Paul was really saying.

I have done a lot of work to learn more about 1 Cor. 6:9-11 since it is so commonly brought up in connection to the issue of homosexuality. Gal. 5:19 is also similar so I will attempt to respond to those two passages. It is really hard to do that quickly or in a few words.

> The passages I'd like to address here are the passage I quoted above and Galatians 5:19-21.

> The acts of the sinful nature are obvious: sexual immorality, impurity and debauchery; idolatry and witchcraft; hatred, discord, jealousy, fits of rage, selfish ambition, dissensions, factions and envy; drunkenness, orgies, and the like. I warn you, as I did before, that those who live like this will not inherit the kingdom of God.

I believe sanctification (the life changes He brings on as a result of the gospel) is an ongoing process in all of our lives. None of us can say we are without sin. Many of us can say we have grown away from many sins as a result of God's intervention in our lives. We are hopefully better today as a result of His work. But thankfully, I understand that Christ's redemption has covered all of my sinfulness from birth and on into the future.

I do not believe in completed work today theology with regards to my temporal life here on earth. I am, with His help, improving each day. However, I will not be completely changed until I see Him face to face. Therefore, I will struggle with various sins off and on throughout the duration of my life. One of those sins may be rebelling against some things that I know are right but just don't want to face them now! But I also understand Christ has forgiven rebellion too.

Having said all of that, I am NOT, hear me now, NOT saying that sin is OK minimizing its affects on our lives. Sin behavior is harmful, negative, divisive, challenging, and God clearly warns us to heed His words and make an attempt to stay from it, with His help and our submission. But we must be very clear about what God does in light of the fact that we do sin.

> You, my brothers and sisters, were called to be free.
> But do not use your freedom to indulge the flesh; rather,
> serve one another humbly in love. Galatians 5:13

I am not saying to give hearty approval to something. My objective is not to forget the scriptural truths about God's desires for our life and relationships. And by the way, the jury remains unclear on some of the things we think are set in stone. I'm rather going through how to respond to people here on earth, which includes myself, who are trying to wrestle through our earthly lives.

To understand this passage we MUST first understand that Paul's letter is addressed to the church in Corinth. This is VERY important! He is writing to Christian believers.

Secondly, in chapter 6, verse 9 he changes to address another audience:

"But to the wicked,(or the unrighteous), I say this."

This means that through the next paragraph he is speaking about those who DO NOT know Jesus. This is VITAL to understanding the next few verses. In the context of the Greek language He has given a list of outward signs so as to say, those who do not know Jesus, who act in habitual patterns like this. It then says they will not inherit the kingdom of heaven.

Something else we must consider. The list of behaviors is not intended to be an inclusive or exclusive list. It is more of a list of examples of those around them who do not know Christ that exemplify the unrighteous people Paul is referring to. As humans, we want things in nice neat packages. If this list were an exclusive list than maybe I am off the hook if I didn't do some of the things listed. I can also stare down at those that are on the list because their behavior is in the list. Paul didn't intend it this way.

Another point is that theologians all over this issue tend to argue the issue of homosexuality with attempt to define the Greek words, "arsenokoitai" and "malakos". This is problematic for many reasons. First, there simply does not seem to be a consensus on what either of those words really mean nor how the many definitions seem to apply to our lives today. I am sure in Paul's day he had something very specific in mind that everyone understood. But, 2000 years later, we do not clearly understand it. To attempt to define something that is not clearly understood and then apply our own interpretation to it can cause all kind of havoc. And it has. It seems that how these words are translated often has more to do with preconceptions and convictions of the readers rather than the sense of the original Greek language.

I think the main problem is that regardless of how they are defined, Paul's list in this passage is not the point of the passage. Therefore we can argue about the list but never get to the point. We can also argue about what it means to gossip, how far is too far in adultery? We can try to define what it means to be a slanderer and when our back door discussions will cross the line. Our discussion about the real meaning of the list is all tied to are we good enough or have we crossed the line? We often want to know if we have gone so far as to lose our precious salvation, are all a distraction from the amazing message Paul has to give us.

We can also get into a discussion about how we do all struggle with so many common things, but many within the Christian community will say, but what about repentance? I have struggled with adultery but I've repented. Okay, if you want to go that route, what about greed? Have we all repented of greed? Not in America! So, do the greedy inherit the kingdom of God? Is their salvation in threat of being lost? Let's be honest. With regard to this passage, many hit the topic of homosexuality with a heavy hand while they themselves are not repentant for the hoarding of worldly goods that they are unwilling to lose or let go of.

In its original context and language it would be more understood like this:

> "Believers in Corinth, there are those who don't know Jesus around you and they act like this. They do things like lie, cheat, steal, hold onto worldly goods, and are sexually out on a limb. They don't seem to know life any differently. You know people like that and you do some of these things yourself. Don't hold on to an identity that hangs on your behaviors. If someone hasn't imparted my gift of redemption to their lives, they will not enter my eternal kingdom. But for you, you know and understand my gospel. I really want you to live honestly through your new identity and restored image in Christ."

It is obvious to me that the real context of what Paul is saying is directly connected to whether or not a person has a real saving relationship with God. Of course the unrighteous won't go to heaven! He is using them as an example to make a point. But he goes on to return to his audience, the church. He says, "But, that is not who you are!" He affirms their relationship with Jesus, their salvation, and says to kindle their position in Christ as being washed, sanctified, by Jesus Christ. He is charging them to remember who they are. So, if you're habitually greedy and haven't seemed to be able to let go, God has covered your sin just as he has the sexually immoral. Or else this passage is null and void.

We all know that Christians all over this planet still struggle with habitual sin patterns like those revealed in the list in verses 9 and 10. Knowing this, says to me, he is not saying that heaven or the kingdom of God is only available to those who are NOT on the list. He is also not saying those who wrestle with, or may even be habitually involved in the things he mentioned there, will not enter eternity with Him.

Paul is challenging their position with God through Jesus death and resurrection, not so much their actions. He is saying, "recognize Who you belong to!" In doing so, you will nurture a relationship with the One who loves you so that your lives will continue down the path of sanctification. If we remain overly connected in the old identity we will likely continue to function out of the shame of the old identity.

He then says, "all things are permissible" but not "beneficial". This is a profound truth. So profound that Paul repeats it twice. Think just a minute about the freedom He speaks of here. He is calling them to further maturity in their actions. As a more mature adult He is calling us to ask ourselves, is this beneficial? Christ still loves you, is still at work in your life and will complete the work He has begun. However, He is charging us to grow in making better decisions along the way.

In Christ, we are absolutely free.

Oh, boy, this is where it gets sticky. Either God gave us a free will or He didn't. I believe He did. I see this as one of the most amazing differences between God and humans. He is able to allow us total freedom and yet still love us completely. He will certainly allow consequences for our bad choices. It is through this that we grow into more maturity. He does not control our lives. So, we are absolutely free to do with our lives as we want to. None of our choices will in any way remove God's love for us. This is one of the most difficult things for me to understand. We are so used to conditional love from other humans it is hard for us to embrace a God that loves us differently.

But in our freedom, we also have the freedom to choose to serve Him. Will we follow Him sacrificially? If we do not get that fundamental truth, our assumptions may lead us to stray from Him, fearing his retribution based upon our failed attempts to act appropriately. Moralism seems to please our human senses. We like to check off the boxes of what we do right and what they do wrong.

> Paul comes back to the same message in his letter to the Galatians:

> You, my brothers and sisters, were called to be free. But do not use your freedom to indulge the flesh[a]; rather, serve one another humbly in love. **Galatians 5:13**

Our church communities are far too full of performance expectations and sin management. We are trapped in a legalism of expectations that keep us weak, immature, and fearful of a God that we believe may be a dictator. We may sense He is ready at any moment to remove His hand, close His heart, and maybe even shut us out. That is if we don't act right.

I now realize that Christ does not hold a hammer over my head waiting to tromp on me if I make the wrong move. I have come to realize a fuller love from Him that is truly as the bible says, unconditional.

I'm starting to gain a better understanding of all of this. If I make the mistake of going against His desires, overt or covert, He loves me, accepts me and offers me His hand. He will be there with me to work with me along the way. No matter how long it takes. He is the divine surgeon who will remain with me through the end of this life and usher me into the next with His abundant grace.

My only option at this point is to love others with that same love. This doesn't mean I will not approach someone with a challenge to do better. If I have built a relationship with them, laid a foundation of trust, I will know when it is appropriate to speak with them as a brother to help them see things through the eyes of Christ that may help them grow.

Paul goes on in his letter to urge believers to consider their sexuality and to recognize that the body is the temple of the Holy Spirit. He lines out for us the deeper motivation to walk in righteousness that is imparted by the gospel. He is exhorting us to consider our lives and our choices.

Galatians 5:19-21

He starts by saying, "acts of the sinful nature." I do not have a sinful nature any longer! I am a new creature in Christ. I have a new heart, a new identity, a new motivation for life! Oh, this doesn't mean I don't have the flaws of humanity. I do wrong things, but these are because of the humanity I live in today. God's new nature is working in me day by day throughout my lifetime. As I read this passage, I see it as a repeated message from Paul. Know who you are! Walk in your new identity! Recognize the differences that are in you as opposed to those who do not know Christ and walk them out! It is NOT a statement of conditions for salvation. And it is a call to maturity. But it is NOT a call to performance based religion.

Again, he is relating to what the unredeemed are like and if you take into account the entire chapter 5, it is saying "we are free." Don't take this freedom lightly, but we are free. It speaks to legalism as the enemy. Submitting to the law as though through it, you will be sanctified by doing the right things. It reiterates the message of the gospel:

> For the entire law is fulfilled in keeping this one command: Love your neighbor as yourself. Galatians 5:14

We Are Free in Christ!

There are several other passages where homosexuality is mentioned. I moved on through them just as I have this one. I have found that the bible is not as clear on men or women having a loving and faithful relationship as I had always thought. There is room for discussion and further study. It appears to me that the jury is still out on this one.

The Gay - Ex-gay Divide

March 2011

Dear John,

I recently read a blog that appeared to say that there is a growing public disagreement between the gay affirming community and the ex-gay community. I know there has always been division there but it seems to be heating up.

Are they both Christian in focus? Isn't the gospel the main thing we should be putting our energy into? It appears to me that they are more interested in how someone is acting rather than seeking to be at work in pursuing the Great Commission.

In our day, it seems there are many who are missing out on the tremendous grace of God as unto salvation. Doesn't God's word say something about division and arguing about these kinds of things?

Joan S.

Dear Joan,

I tend to agree with you and would like to address this in a more public manner. There is a great divide between the gay community and those who ascribe to the ex-gay way of thinking. The ex-gays are saying God will, and needs to, provide healing for their brokenness. The gay Christian community is saying there is nothing to be healed in relationship to their homosexuality. Some on the ex-gay side can even say that if someone doesn't agree that homosexual behavior is a sin, they may not even be Christian!

Can Christians disagree on biblical definitions of what is sin and what is not sin and still follow Jesus Christ together? Does one's definition of any particular sin determine whether or not someone is in fact in Christ?

This is not a new division, This is an age old divide that has kept the Christian community distracted for over 2000 years. Can we eat pork? Do all male followers of Christ have to be circumcised? Can a Christian regularly drink wine? Is slavery an acceptable way to work our fields? Can someone be divorced and remain in fellowship? These have all been issues within the church that have caused huge conflicts throughout the years.

Can someone be homosexual in heart and in action and still be an active, God glorifying Christian?

I am not the one who can make that decision. Whether a person identifies as ex-gay or gay , they have one thing in common: they both experience attractions and relationship desires for those of their same gender. These desires will very likely never go away and will be something they must learn to accept as part of their life experience. It is between them and God to figure out what to do with the desires that rage within them. You may not understand or accept this, but for many who come to a place of saying "I'm gay" can bring them to a wonderful freedom from condemnation through Christ.

If a person is in fact in Christ, then this is a spiritual reality. When a person is a Christian, I believe God says "there is therefore no condemnation for those who are in Christ Jesus" (Rom. 8:1), none!

Is there any distinction between those who choose to go the ex-gay route, or a gay affirming one that would void one's faith in Christ? One may say that an unrepentant perspective of homosexuality would clearly set them apart from a faith in Christ, but I would say that's not so.

While some may be in a posture of believing any homosexual act is sin, and some may embrace same sex committed relationships; if they are in Christ, are we not still one Church, one Body?

Sadly, many have lumped homosexual people into one big negative bag. There are those who believe that all homosexuals are sick, sinful, and in need of healing for their poor broken lives. Think about this for just a minute. How might you feel if you were a believer in Christ who had felt His wonder and awe enter your life and you happened to be gay? You hear that you need to be free of your attractions and become heterosexual in order to really know Christ and begin to wonder if Christ is enough. I would likely feel helpless, discouraged, challenged and confused. On one hand you hear that salvation is in Christ alone, but it seems that others are saying there are conditions to having a relationship with Him.

As I reflect on the opportunity to be at The Evangelical Network conference with people who celebrate Christ and believe that having a faithful committed relationship with the same sex is acceptable to God, I cannot ignore what I saw. Now, before you stop reading and try to judge this scenario, I want you to hear something I observed.

This crowd of people, about 180 of them, had one really important thing in common. They were proclaiming to know Jesus, His sacrifice and His resurrection. They were excited to know that He loved them enough to embrace them wholly and completely as they are. These folks were passionate about having experienced the gospel and its power in their lives.

I was invited to hear a report on their ministries and mission efforts. The summation of what I heard was that they were excited about, and praying for, their outreach to the gay community to share the gospel of redemption through Jesus Christ. I was humbled and amazed! I thought to myself, "What is it that motivates these people to be so excited about sharing the gospel?" I looked back over conferences and church meetings I had been to in the past. I was aware that there was a blatant absence of a passion to share the gospel to those who didn't know.

In contrast, there was an overt message within recovery meetings and ex-gay conferences where the message was predominantly "we are all broken and we need to get our sorry lives together so that maybe we will be able to minister to others." Sadly, the emphasis was more on getting our act together than the thankfulness of how much Jesus loves us and wanted us to share His love with others.

If Christians are told over and over that their hearts are deceitful and wicked and that they are broken, where is redemption in Christ? Is it not a slap in the face of the torturous sacrifice and a victorious resurrection of Christ to continue berating ourselves and others who are believers in Jesus with this out-of-context quote?

I was involved in ex-gay recovery ministry for over twenty years. I think one of the greatest regrets I have from those years is the many times I have tried to tell people they were broken lives and that they had a deceived heart. I did so thinking I was quoting Scripture and telling them the truth.

> The heart is deceitful above all things and beyond cure.
> Who can understand it? Jer. 17:9

Oh, I know that we make many mistakes and there are things we could use a good spiritual healing from. I also know that we are a work in progress. But, something I have come to realize is that when the Holy Spirit makes us new, creates in us a clean new heart, He has done an amazing and awesome work in us. As David cried out, "Create in me a clean heart, O God; and renew a right spirit within me" (Ps. 51) not only was his prayer answered, but also our prayers have been answered as well, through Christ.

> The tongue of the righteous is choice silver, but the heart
> of the wicked is of little value Prov. 10:20

But, who are the wicked? Some bible versions refer to the wicked as the unrighteous those who are not in relationship with Jesus Christ. But for those who are, God has given them the new heart. Therefore, to say that a believer in Jesus has a wicked or deceived heart denies God's restorative work in our hearts and lives.

How does this apply today? It has often been said that homosexuals have a wicked and deceived heart. Some people even go so far as to say they are an abomination. Really? Can we say that this means they are not saved – any of them? If a man has a wicked and deceived heart, then that says to me that he does not know Jesus. If someone has come to salvation, then God has softened his heart of stone into a heart of flesh. He has given him a new, healed heart. He is no longer wicked or unrighteous, but rather, he is righteous by the blood of Christ.

Having a tremendous burden for the gay community, I can see how, as Christians, we can continue to wound those we say we want to help. When we continue to proclaim to them they are broken, deceived, unsalvageable, it is like putting poison into the medicine bottle that we are hoping will provide better health. We are inadvertently tearing down the work of Christ while we are proclaiming its value.

Where is our focus? Are we so busy judging one another's lives that we are missing the point? Is our focus on a Jesus that loves us deeply, saves us radically, renews our hearts miraculously, and asks us to tell others?

We need to get our act together and quit shooting each other with our critical, dividing ways. God can and will do an amazing work amongst us if we are willing. If not, then we can waste a lot of time and energy trying to do what only God can do. He, and only He, is the judge of our lives. His word is very clear about this kind of division.

But avoid foolish controversies and genealogies and arguments and quarrels about the law because these are unprofitable and useless. Warn a divisive person once, and then warn them a second time. After that, have nothing to do with them. You may be sure that such people are warped and sinful; they are self-condemned. Titus 3:9-11

Take this as a warning! Stop arguing about this kind of stuff! This isn't saying to have nothing more to do with homosexuals. It says to stop hanging around those who are spending so much time arguing and quarreling about it.

Are we trying to cut off the foreskins of those God says don't need it done? Are we trying to grab the wine bottles out of the hands of those God says are free to drink from them? And what about those who say "I am gay"? Are we spending more time trying to tell homosexuals who know Jesus how sick they are? Or, are we embracing them, along with their gifts and talents, into the body of Christ with us while trusting the rest to God?

"Oh, boy, John. You're really out there now!"

I'm really trying to trust my relationship with Jesus more and more. I've never been more excited about knowing Him than I am today. I've never felt freer in Him than I do now. His freedom doesn't mean permissiveness; rather to me it means an opportunity to see Him more clearly, hear his heart more intensively, and respond accordingly.

So if the Son sets you free, you will be free indeed. John 8:36

I want everyone to know Christ, and Him crucified. I continue to pray that God sends me to share this good news with anyone who will listen. Do you have the same desire I do? Then we are of one mind and one Spirit regarding this matter. Let God work the other things out in His way, His time, and for His purpose.

To those who are gay and to those who are struggling with these words, this is my heart and my prayer:

> God loves you deeply, completely, radically and
> redemptively! He embraces you wholly and loves you
> with absolute abandon! He has given you abundant talents,
> amazing gifts, incredible discernment and wants you to
> explore all of the wonderful ways He wants to use you
> to share His love with others.

I choose to walk alongside you in this incredible journey of our life in Christ. I want to see the miracles He does through you. I want to pray with you, worship with you, and embrace the Holy Spirit's joy together beside you.

If we find each other to lack something, I pray we will share from our abundance with each other. If we find we are walking a crooked *path I pray we will provide assistance in direction when needed. If we fall and need a stick or cane, I pray we will provide it for one another.*

If either of us becomes quarrelsome, I pray we will gently warn each other and separate for a season if we don't have the grace to stop. If we hurt each other, it is my hope we will tell each other and seek to forgive.

Where Christ is uplifted between two or more of us, He is present; and I pray we will enjoy wonderful fellowship.

I received this email from Europe from someone who had read a recent article on my blog called The Gay /Ex-gay Divide. In my ongoing discovery of the incredible freedom that we are provided in Christ, this man's story exemplifies changes in his life that have occurred. He has received a loving relationship with Jesus as his church has accepted him right where he is with no agenda.

What I appreciate most is the journey without an expected timeline of growth. This man is following the Lord's leading in his life. The message here is that God will do His work, in His time, and in His way.

God's work in any of our lives cannot be duplicated and sold off for someone else to follow. It is unique to who we are and where we are in life's journey. For Robert, he clearly describes some of his journey below.

Hello, John,

Thank you for writing the article on your website blog about the battle between the gay and ex-gay community!

I believe the church has missed a lot of chances to reach out to the gay community. Although I am on the side of literal interpretation of the scripture . I can still get angry about the judgmental and, in my opinion, totally stupid attitude of a lot of fundamental straight Christians who do not know WHAT it is like when one is dealing with same sex attraction. I get a lot of support in my church, fortunately.

When I dedicated my life to Christ about a year ago, after about twenty years of hedonistic plunging into everything gay. I told the pastor everything about me and my life, and I did not hold back. Sometimes I told him to brace himself for what he would hear from me. But I needed to do this in order to have no secrets or secret places in my heart anymore. I learned that secrets can grow and take hold of one's life after growing.

Now from my pastor and other people in church, there was no judgment at all…nothing…. When I recall the conversations with him, I can recall only a listening ear and understanding…and then a hand on my shoulder during prayer. I was welcomed into his house and his family. I had dinners at his place together with the partner I had at that time because they wanted to welcome my partner too.

I knew if God would change my life...my partner had a right to know God as well. My conviction that homosexuality is a sin actually came from what I read in scripture and from the gentle voice inside of me from the Holy Spirit . My church friends never pressed me into anything.

This was such a relief for me, to be welcomed and accepted in the midst of this Christian community. Just people showing me Jesus through their lives and their attitude. That love ...that unconditional love.

God has worked miracles in the past year. Although what I feel is the thorn in my flesh comes up now and then, and sometimes a lot, but I feel so free. I experience God so close. God speaks to me. God's spirit shows me inner wounds that He wants to heal and take care of. Sometimes stuff I did not even know was there. Sometimes when I am walking alone in the woods or driving the car, the Holy Spirit has His private pastoral sessions with me, showing me all these things. I feel so privileged. Sometimes it's like being in a desert. Then it seems I am all alone. But then I hold on. I don't want to give up. I don't want to let go of this God.

I am still officially in a relationship with my partner. But the physical stuff between us has stopped. We are now good friends. We have been together for fourteen years. Slowly and gently God is leading us into separate ways. We are not there yet. But I am so thankful for God's grace in this broke me...it tore down the walls around my heart ... it is the most forceful power.

A New Friend, Robert

"This is What Love In Action Looks Like"

A Film Premier - San Francisco, CA

June 2011

Some good friends of mine held a prayer meeting for a weekend trip to San Francisco for the Frameline Film Festival. One of my personal requests was that I would not feel alone. I had contacted two people to meet with me while I was there but had only one confirmation for Saturday. I also asked them to pray for our critics and enemies. In the New Testament, Jesus and others give us the exhortation to pray for our enemies, so in this situation I felt it appropriate to follow that model.

Sitting at the Memphis airport waiting to board my flight for Detroit, I received a phone call. It was from a new friend named Jeff who contacted me a year ago to talk with me about his story. He told me that he had just happened to go to his FaceBook account earlier that day and read my website blog. He looked on my page and found out that I was coming to San Francisco where he lives.

Jeff asked if I might have some time to talk with him while I was there. I told him I had Friday evening and Sunday afternoon and evening open. He said he wanted to meet with me on Sunday afternoon so we put it down. I was hoping he would say Friday because I didn't really want to just sit around after getting into San Francisco. A few minutes later, he called me back and asked if I wanted to have dinner with him on Friday. I was really glad he was open and began to relax about the weekend.

So I took the BART subway train from the airport to San Francisco. Out of the subway station I walked just half a block and saw my hotel! How easy was that? I found the bed and breakfast type of hotel to be clean, comfortable, and practical. It was the cheapest hotel I could find in San Francisco! I had also booked the hotel because it was just one block from the theater where the film was going to be presented.

When Jeff called to give me directions to where he was going to meet me for dinner, it was just a few blocks from my hotel. That was great! So, at dinner time I walked out of the hotel and found an easy and quite beautiful walk to meet him. I stood on the street for a little while, and then he called and said he was waiting inside the restaurant.

I found Jeff to be very hospitable, kind, and interesting. Jeff began to tell me that he had been involved with Love In Action in the early 1980's. Since I arrived at Love In Action in the mid-1980's we found common ground in people we knew. So we shared our history, and we related in our journey with homosexuality and Christ. After several hours and lots of easy conversation, we said goodnight; and I walked back to my hotel.

Morgan Fox, the creator of the film we were going to see on Saturday, had texted me with information about meeting that morning for break-fast with him and his friends. So Saturday morning I got up and looked at the map to find that the restaurant was just a few blocks away as well. I was familiar with the location since I had walked by it the night before, so again I felt quite comfortable with the plan. Morgan's partner was along on the trip, so at breakfast we met for the first time. I found him to be quiet but very pleasant.

I was feeling anxious as I sat there. I was in San Francisco at a LBGT film festival to see a screening of a film that focused on a critical view of the ministry I had been involved in for twenty-two years. I tried to come up with what was in my heart but found it hard to think and didn't have any idea what to expect. So our conversation at breakfast was pleasant but distracted due to all of our being in thought about what was coming.

I had arranged with another friend, named Mick, whom I had known from the early 1990's to get together on Saturday afternoon. He contacted me and said he would be coming to the film. I was glad to see a familiar face when I arrived at the theater for sure.

As Mick and I sat down at the theater, he began to ask me about my recent history regarding the protests at Love In Action as well as what has gone on since my departure from Love In Action in 2008. As I talked, I realized that God was preparing my heart for what I might say when Morgan and I gave our opening statements at the presentation. I was amazed that God had provided me with the opportunity to process my thoughts with Mick in preparation for the film.

Then I looked up and saw another familiar face. He had made a mad dash across town to be at the film. It was so good to see him. Earlier on Saturday morning I was chatting on FaceBook with Ryan who was in Love In Action in the early 1990's. Amazingly, my wife was chatting with Ryan at the same time! We arranged for breakfast on Sunday. I had contacted another friend, who knew Ryan as well, for a Sunday breakfast; but it wasn't confirmed as yet.

There was one film that was going to be shown prior to Morgan's film, and I was curious to see it. It was titled *All We Need is Love*. It was a film about an 11 year old girl who lived in a world where being gay was the norm. As she grew, she realized she was heterosexual and began to discover how hard it was to be heterosexual in a gay world. As the film moved on she was teased, bullied, and beat up. Her parents didn't seem to understand what she was going through, and she felt alienated and unheard.

As this film was moving along, I began to feel fearful and anxious. I thought, "Oh, boy, why did they have to show this film right before our film. This will raise the defensive emotional level in this audience, and I could get slaughtered when they show Morgan's film." His film focused on a youth who was experiencing the same internal conflicts that little girl felt , and his parents took him to Love In Action when he didn't want to go. I actually came to the realization that I could get accosted maybe even physically beat up here. I just prayed asking for God's grace no matter what. I had to go through this and also had to trust Him in it.

So, when Morgan and I got up to give an opening statement, from my recollection, this is what I said.

> "In 2005, a huge protest uprooted my life. My entire world was rocked; and through this one event I began to evaluate my spiritual, emotional, moral, and ethical positions. Much like when Jesus came into our world and challenged the very core of our existence, Morgan Fox came into my world with this protest and challenged me deeply." At that point I had tears in my eyes and heart. Then we sat down and the film began.

I listened to every word in the film intently. I paid special attention to my own words. There were excerpts from media interviews as well as some from interviews with Morgan. My reactions swung from embarrassment to confidence. I realized that this one film was taking me through a season of my life when Jesus did some of the deepest work in my own heart that has been done in my entire Christian walk.

As the film ended, the crew from the first film, and the folks from Morgan's crew, including me, walked to the stage. The audience was then asked for questions. After a couple of logistical questions about where the films could be seen again and how they could get them for themselves, the audience turned to questions for me.

To be honest, I don't actually remember the questions or much of what I said. Two people filmed the question time, so I'll be able to find that out at a later date what was said. All I remember is that several people spoke to the negative issues represented but affirmed my being there to stand with Morgan and to represent the changes in my heart relating to what God had done in me. It was all quite respectful and appropriate.

Afterwards, there was a line of people to speak to me, and we had to move our discussion out to the street. Two people stood out to me. One was a lady who came to me in tears. "John, your honesty and your heart changes along with your apology have healed a deep wound in my heart." She hugged me closely and said, "Thank you so much." Then a man came up to me and talked with me vulnerably about how he had felt alienated from the church. He spoke of his family's rejection and the losses he had experienced. My heart went out to him, and I told him to contact me if he felt I could be of any encouragement for him.

Phew, no one beat me up. No one was rude. No one was angry with me. Our prayers for our enemies had been answered. I am certain there must have been those in the audience that didn't like me and were angry, but the Lord had kept them at bay; and I was thankful.

As we all prepared to go to lunch, Ryan came up to me to give me his reactions. He said, "John, I had no idea you had gone through such a change in your heart. I came here to see you just because I loved you and your wife. You took me into your lives when I wasn't able to see my own family. I felt a little anxious coming to see you because I figured you were going to challenge me with something 'out of love.' But I just put that aside and decided to see you out of being friends even if we disagreed." He then told me of his shock when he heard my apology and that I had discovered a new perspective of grace. I was humbled that this man would come to see me even though he felt challenged by the potential of disunity.

Mick and Ryan came with us to lunch. On one side of the table were Morgan and his friends; on the other side were my friends with me. As the discussion began, Ryan took the lead and began to ask questions and make comments about our history from years ago. Since Morgan and his friends had worked for so long on the documentary, they found it interesting to meet these men with a Love In Action history.

After lunch, Mick and I went off to spend some quality one-on-one time at my hotel. As we talked, our hearts were knit together once again. We were really good friends when we had lived near each other in the early 1990's but hadn't spoken at all since then. Mick told his story of how he had come to accept his homosexuality and that he had been with his partner for fourteen years now. He talked about their involvement in a home bible study and how connected they were to their Christian fellowship and friends. I told him how my life had been and the things I had experienced through the years. I think we were both captured by the grace of God in each of our lives.

After a couple of hours we walked several blocks to have dinner together. As we got to Chow restaurant and sat down by the window along the sidewalk, something stirred in my heart. I looked around me and saw about 90 percent of the people were gay. Here I was in San Francisco, just a few blocks from the Castro, the gay district. I was across the bay from where Love In Action was founded and had I lived for eight years. I was captured by this dichotomy and the current situation.

As I looked around at the diversity of those in the restaurant and those who were walking by the window, I realized for the first time I didn't feel fearful of these people. Rather I saw them as men, women, young and old, just people. I recognized that I felt a kind of camaraderie with them and a love for them.

Through the twenty-two years I was involved with Love In Action, I would often say I loved the homosexual community. But that night I realized that I had loved with conditions on my love. I felt softened towards a homosexual if they were seeking Love In Action's help, but when I thought of homosexuals in San Francisco I just felt darkness, a type of pungency that kept me away. I saw San Francisco as a dark, horrific place where people were lost, rebellious, and anti-God!

Suddenly something in my soul said, "How will you ever encourage them if you don't love them?" That's it! I didn't love them. I had a boundary, a barrier, a wall that I was unwilling to see through or climb. But this day, once again, Morgan Fox was used to break down another wall. His film brought me to San Francisco where God would reveal to me my own heart of judgment and showed me His heart of grace. I was in tears in front of Mick as I told him what had just occurred to me.

We finished dinner, and Mick walked with me back to my hotel on his way to his car. We embraced and talked of how wonderful it was to know each other again in this season of our life.

I felt fulfilled from the day. I sensed an amazing dose of God's heart and His grace and mercy upon me. I felt protected and connected rather than fearful and alone.

Sunday morning came. Ryan sent me a text and said that our friend Michael was going to meet us for breakfast. I was elated. I always loved Michael but hadn't seen him for fifteen or more years either. When I got to the restaurant, Ryan had just arrived. When we sat down he said, "John, I had to do a pretty good sales job to get Michael to come this morning. He was feeling angst and asked me if I knew why John Smid wanted to see us. He told me that Michael was tenuous about our meeting just like he was the day before.

I felt grieved about what he said. I thought I always loved them with unconditional love. But as he shared of their fears of being with me I realized that they didn't see the same unconditional love that I thought I was showing them. Obviously, in their angst, they felt conditions and expectations might be in play here.

Ryan was single and had accepted his homosexuality. He is deeply involved in events connected to the San Francisco gay community. Michael had also accepted his homosexuality and had been with a long term partner for over six years.

When Michael arrived, I began by telling him that I wanted to put him at ease. I told him of how God had broken my heart open for the gay community and that I was not here to confront him for his homosexuality or for his having a partner. As I sat there looking at a man I had known so well over fifteen years earlier, I saw his soul and could clearly look past anything that was on the surface of his life. I saw the same man I had known and loved earlier in our lives.

During our conversation, Ryan mentioned to me that he had chosen to divest his gifts and passions in fund raising and support of organizations he felt were doing really good things. He said that years ago he felt alienated from the church but still had a heart for missions and reaching people. So since he couldn't find a place that would accept him as a homosexual in a Christian place, he found other places to fit. He talked of how the Gay Games of San Francisco embraced him and wanted him to help them. He felt significant. But along the way he had distanced himself from any public or outward connection to God, but he knew that God was still with him inside.

Michael began to tell me his story. He said that when he was in his early twenties, he remembers "hiring Jesus" to fix him. He said that when Jesus didn't seem to do what He had been hired to do, he became disenchanted with God and just walked away. He came to accept that he was gay and met his partner. He said he hadn't been in any church or read a bible in many years.

As I heard their stories my heart broke. Here were these two men that I loved dearly years ago. When I knew them, their hearts were expectant for God to move and were soft towards His mercy. But when they got discouraged and lost hope, they went away; and those who said they loved them abandoned them. They left them because these two men weren't performing as the others wanted them to, so they just virtually left them on the street.

I was one of those who did that. I remember distinctly when I heard that Ryan was living in San Francisco. I was frustrated with his choices and just accused him of being rebellious. I thought, "Why would anyone who is a Christian with homosexual desires want to live in that city if they were pursuing God?" I didn't really care about Ryan; all I was interested in was someone agreeing with me and following my expectations. And Michael? I had lost touch with him. When I found him on FaceBook I saw that he was with a same sex partner and living in San Francisco.

This day, sitting in a diner on Market Street in San Francisco, I was in their living room of life. As I saw their faces and heard their hearts, how could I possibly be judgmental about their lives? I felt nothing but respect for their honesty and was privileged to hear their stories.

So, God seemed to speak to me and I looked at Michael in the eyes and said, "Michael, I want you to know something. I want you to hear the truth. You ARE God's best. Not your flesh or your life choices, YOU! You, Michael, Are God's absolute BEST!"

I followed with an apology. "Michael, Ryan, Please forgive me for anything I have said, done, or represented that has ever communicated to you that you are anything less than loved by God deeply, richly, and that you are both His absolute BEST!"

I was amazed and almost wept during our conversation. I saw an aspect of God's amazing grace at work right before my eyes! The changes in the hearts of these two men were almost instantaneous. I began to reflect on something that Paul said in the book of Romans, because through Christ Jesus the law of the Spirit who gives life has set you free from the law of sin and death.

We went on to spend the next hour or so encouraging each other in our lives and in our faith. We dug into the truth of God's Spirit in each of us regardless of all of the shortcomings and imperfections in our lives of flesh. We talked of how God's desires for us are always for good and that He never leaves us nor forsakes us.

Michael then told me something he remembered from almost twenty years ago. He said, "John, I remember your telling me that I was a Jewel and to never forget my testimony. You told me that people were always drawn to me and would remember me."

I said, "Michael, how cool is that? It is true! You are a "Jewel" and I have never forgotten you. And… this is your testimony. The dark times, the invisible times of Jesus, and the good times—your life is your testimony. You are on the Journey of Christ!"

He said he and his partner were moving to Southern California and that he was looking forward to a new beginning in life. He said that this conversation had given him hope that maybe his new beginning would include renewing his relationship with Christ.

I sighed, and then Ryan said that he also was looking to a new beginning with God. His plans were to hike the Appalachian Trail next spring and that he was looking forward to finding God there and gaining a renewed life. He talked about how being with me this weekend and hearing my story of God's grace had caused him to see the dominoes in his own life begin to fall down rapidly this weekend.

FaceBook played a very significant role in this weekend. Connecting with friends from California became an impetus for me to go to San Francisco for the festival. Throughout the weekend, it was a communication tool to keep me in touch with several friends I was meeting with as well as some comments after the meetings. Mick, my friend who came to the film, wrote me and said he felt deeply encouraged and renewed in his own faith through our conversation on Saturday. All three men told me how much they looked forward to keeping in touch and following through with what God had begun this weekend.

I went back to my hotel just for a short break to get ready to meet my other friend Jeff from Friday evening. He was bringing along with him a friend who was in town for the weekend. This man, Samuel, had been in Love In Action in the early 1980's with Jeff. So, we met at a hang out on Market Street in the middle of the gay community. As I sat there, I felt a little uncomfortable because it was more of a social gay atmosphere. But I prayed and continued to see God's grace there too.

As Jeff and Samuel and I got together, Jeff had brought two other people with him. They were a heterosexual married couple who just happened to live in Omaha, my home town. How curious is that? As we began to talk, they brought up that they knew there were Christian programs that targeted gay youth to try to change them. I said, "That would have been me." I went on to say that from what I knew we were the only program for youth and that the film I was involved with was critical of that very program. How interesting?

Then Jeff, Samuel and I went to dinner and reminisced about all of the friends from way back when and caught each other up to date on those we had updates on.

When I got back to my hotel I realized that God had sent Jeff at the last minute to be my host for the weekend. Bookends from Friday night and Sunday night, Jeff brought security and comfort to the angst of being alone in San Francisco. God had removed my enemies. God had provided incredible connections with others for encouragement and support. I had all of a couple of free hours of time in all three days. He broke open a new part of my heart for the gay community and showed me the value of His grace at work miraculously! So, we'll see what is next. This is only a milepost on my personal journey.

Rediscovering Grace Together

July 2011

> In those days John the Baptist came, preaching in the wilderness of Judea and saying, "Repent, for the kingdom of heaven has come near."
>
> This is he who was spoken of through the prophet Isaiah: Matthew 3:1-3
>
> From that time on Jesus began to preach, "Repent, for the kingdom of heaven has come near." Matthew 4:17

"REPENT!"

This word brings a negative history of screaming to my mind. As I think of the itinerant preachers along the countryside or those inside the large auditoriums having laid before us the "turn or burn" mentality, it certainly left questions in my mind about what John the Baptist or Jesus meant in these passages. What has often come to my mind with the word repent is that it is connected to behaviors or habits that some would say need to stop. I certainly haven't felt particularly loved when I hear those words in my mind. I am sure you may not either. But think about this.

During a recent bible study with some of my gay friends, where we were reading through the book of Matthew we were digging our way through the first four chapters. With resource books, lots of discussion, and sharing our own observations, something profound hit us.

Repent? What are these writers trying to tell those who are reading their words? As we grappled through these words, we discussed how we had always thought of repentance as changing something in our behavior. To quit a negative habit or to stop doing something that was wrong. It seemed we all agreed that our concept of repentance was connected to actions. We also agreed that it was usually attached to someone pointing the finger at us with expectations, or, sad to say, judgment.

As we looked these passages over and over, we realized that it was more likely connected to a heart change. It had to do with recognizing the bigger picture of the gospel where John was asking those around him to get ready for a new kingdom, a kingdom where Jesus was king. Jesus was following up with a challenge to turn from a worldly kingdom to an eternal kingdom. There was a common thread of something much deeper than just a behavior change or cessation of a habit.

In the Old Testament to repent meant to turn. In the New Testament, it means a complete change of life, a heart change much deeper than just a change in behavior. It's about our heart with God. It's connected to a willingness to see God for who He really is. It's a movement from the kingdom of this world to the kingdom of God.

> "The time has come," he said. "The kingdom of God has come near. Repent and believe the good news!"
> Mark 1:15

Jesus was asking us to relinquish false saviors and false kingdoms and to believe and trust Him. He preached this message to the in group of the Israelites, the Pharisees!

> And whoever does not carry their cross and follow me cannot be my disciple. Luke 14:27

After His statement about loving Him more than even our own families, Jesus is asking us to count the cost of repentance. Turning from the kingdom of this world to the kingdom of God is extremely costly! Interestingly enough, the Pharisees (hmmm, can we say today religious legalists) began to grumble while the sinners and tax collectors began to turn to Him.

> Now the tax collectors and sinners were all gathering around to hear Jesus. But the Pharisees and the teachers of the law muttered, "This man welcomes sinners and eats with them." Luke 15:1-2

Jesus message of repentance was not completely focused on behavior change, but rather it was a calling unto Himself. It is a desire for relationship. It's a calling to a new kingdom.

> John said to the crowds coming out to be baptized by him, "You brood of vipers! Who warned you to flee from the coming wrath? Produce fruit in keeping with repentance. And do not begin to say to yourselves, 'We have Abraham as our father.' For I tell you that out of these stones God can raise up children for Abraham. The ax is already at the root of the trees, and every tree that does not produce good fruit will be cut down and thrown into the fire." Luke 3:7-9

Notice who the brood of vipers was. It was those who were worshiping their religion. He was asking them to consider what the true fruit of repentance was. The good fruit of having a real life relationship with Jesus. Not the outcome of a legalistic religious practice. Jesus was stern with sinners, but He was angry with the Pharisees. Too often repentance is a legalistic, preachy message, not a call to fall in love with the Savior.

As we mulled this over each of us was acutely aware that we had the wrong idea about repentance. We realized we could change our negative views of repentance to one of a loving gift, a wonderful opportunity that is always present.

I remember God showing me that I had a wrong place in my heart regarding people of another race and that He saw them differently than I did. Dealing with judging others is something that is ever present in our lives. However, it doesn't do any good to attempt to change ourselves. It isn't so much about repenting of racism as it is repenting of our unwillingness to see people as God does. Repentance is about turning to God for His perspective, His heart for others, and His heart for me.

Through the last three years the thing that has been working itself deep into my heart is how great God's love is for us, and I've been learning a deeper understanding of His abundant grace. I realize that God's love is really hard to grasp as a human. I also understand that the word grace can mean myriads of things to us and is hard to grasp as well. But, today, I am particularly struck by the way God's grace can change my heart and how it can encourage others.

But God has been revealing to me the way that I had been critical of others and really had not fully understood what God grace is in my own life. Therefore I was not a good reflection of what He likely meant. When I began to grasp God's abundant love for me in a new way, I began to see the changes in my heart towards others. This brought me to a place where I really wanted to reconnect with people I had known years earlier. I really wanted them to know what I had discovered and that I loved them. I wanted to ask them to forgive me for my conditional love for them.

I am acutely aware of how so many people live in such deeply rooted shame. A type of shame that says, "You are damaged goods". This is not from the Spirit of our God, rather from the pit of hell! This shame is so hard to fight against. But, I know that God loves us through our shame and against the common messages sent to us from some people who really don't understand God's grace.

I have had the amazing opportunity to sit with individuals one on one, up front and personal. I am amazed and have almost wept during our conversations. I've seen an aspect of God's amazing grace at work right before my eyes! The changes in their hearts have been almost instantaneous. I began to reflect on something that Paul said in the book of Romans, "...because through Christ Jesus the law of the Spirit who gives life has set you free from the law of sin and death."

During these incredible times together in their own unique ways, these men said they realized they had been estranged from their relationship with God. Each one in his own way talked of how he was struggling to find a place in his faith that would become real and tangible. In many of these meetings there was evidence in the changes in my own heart. I found an ability to listen, to affirm, and to lay judgment down.

I found it very interesting that our bible study seemed to correlate with each of these stories so well. If I had said to any of them "you need to repent" I am sure they would have heard "You are so bad; clean up your act so that God can accept you."

Instead, the only thing in my heart was to let them know how much God loves them right now, today, always. I think that was on John the Baptist's heart, and certainly it is Jesus' heart.

"Repent, for the kingdom of heaven has come near."

I have no doubt today that Jesus was saying to us:

"Here I am! I love you so much; I am going to give my life for you. I have come to let you know that I can become your King if you let me. I can change your heart from a heart of stone to a heart of flesh.

I can bring you a new life that will answer so many questions. I will go in your stead to the Judge and tell Him that I've got you covered from the eternal consequences of your imperfection. I really want you to know that, without me, you will die eternally and I don't want that to happen because I want you to live with me forever!" Now, that sure sounds a lot different from what I had always heard in my head.

> "Turn or burn. Get your life together. STOP THAT!" Or "Clean up your act!"

What I Hear Now

> "Come to me, all you who are weary and burdened, and I will give you rest. Take my yoke upon you and learn from me, for I am gentle and humble in heart, and you will find rest for your souls. For my yoke is easy and my burden is light." Matthew 11:28-30

> Repent, then, and turn to God, so that your sins may be wiped out, that times of refreshing may come from the Lord, and that He may send the Messiah, who has been appointed for you—even Jesus. Acts 3:19-20

I have hope that I will get the opportunity to be a messenger of God's grace to many more whom He wants me to know, to listen to and to love.

After I met with Ryan and Michael for breakfast, we walked outside the diner. I looked across the street and saw that the building was the San Francisco Gay and Lesbian Community Center.

Above the building I saw this little cross rising from the top. I mentioned it to them and said, "Isn't that interesting, a cross on top of that building?" In my heart, I couldn't deny that it was a wonderful symbol of God's love for all people and His desire to be their King!

They said, "Oh, that's a cross on the Baptist church behind the center. I am sure they don't have anything good to say to us."

Well, no matter what anyone wants to say, I believe His endless call for us to join Him for His eternal kingdom, is a call to repentance, a turning and going the opposite direction. But it doesn't start with changing behavior. It starts with a changed heart – and only He can give us that. Once we are His, He can do the fixing just fine.

"John, You Have Deviated From the Truth!"

August 2011

I received a letter from a concerned pastor friend. With his permission I have copied his letter in its entirety and my response below.

Dear John,

Thank you for your e-mails. I must address your recent article entitled, "Can My Gay Friend Be a Christian?"

I feel your love and heart for those in the gay community. The compassion that I sense you have for them is rare and is the love of Christ. You help us all to understand compassion.

I wonder if after you left Love In Action several years ago, you have slowly deviated somewhat from the truth. Somewhere, I believe that the pressure from the gay community has compelled you to create a more accommodating doctrine for gays that will ultimately allow them to feel comfortable in their sin.

You speak about how we all live in opposition to God's desires for our lives every day. I am in agreement with that. Of course, we all do. However, that's different from living in iniquity.

Here is the dilemma: How do we distinguish Christians who struggle with sin from unsaved people who are practicing sin? I believe Paul explains it through his own early struggle with sin before he found victory. Even though he struggled with doing wrong while saved, in Romans 7:15, he states that he hated what he was doing. In verse 16, he acknowledged that God's law is good (holy, righteous).

When people call themselves gay, which God calls sin, then they are saying that God's law or standard is not good. They do not agree with God's standard if they continue to live in their sin and call themselves gay. They have not accepted God's truth.

A Christian should inwardly recognize that God's Word is right, true, and good, and that their sin is wrong. This is the key to distinguishing a sinner from a Christian who struggles with sin. If there is no guilt, conviction, or inward shame when a person commits an act of sin, then this is reason to question his/her salvation. A Christian who still struggles with sin, however, will not want to practice sin.

They trip up occasionally, but they have a desire to stop sinning. They do not feel good inwardly when they sin. The issue comes down to the heart.

> Whosoever committeth sin transgresseth also the law: for sin is the transgression of the law (1 John 3:4).

The person who continuously practices sin is lawless or without God's law. He has no regard, acceptance, agreement, or conviction from the laws of God. This is the sinner who has no guilt, conviction, shame, or hatred for evil, as Paul described in Romans 7.

If a person has made the decision in his/her heart to depart from homosexuality (or any other iniquity for that matter), then he/she will not want to remain in that sin and call himself/herself gay. A Christian cannot still practice being gay; therefore, they cannot call themselves gay. If we fall in a moment of weakness, we repent and keep going. This is one thing. Practicing and continuing to call oneself gay is another. I hope this provides some perspective. I pray that I have not offended you.

Sincerely,

Pastor

Dear Pastor,

First of all, I have read through your letter and I'm pondering your words. I want to make sure you know clearly that your letter did not offend me. I deeply respect that you have taken the time and written me about this.

As I thought about having received your letter one thing that stood out to me clearly, I have always felt loved by you. As long as I have known you, your heart overflows with affirmation, kindness, and certainly I feel connected to you personally. Therefore, I know your letter is coming from that place. I know you love me.

I will attempt to reply to the letter as I find the words to do so. These last two years have been a wonderful season in my life. God has been at work digging into my heart on many levels. When I left Love In Action, I had time to rest and ponder the things of the Lord. After 22 years of managing the wheelhouse of Love In Action, I was completely worn out for sure. I needed to rest in the Lord. I have experienced a long overdue sabbatical of sorts. During this time I have put a lot of prayer and work into hearing from Him about how He would have me to respond to the reality of homosexuality.

I am finally feeling refreshed with new vision, a new understanding of God's love for me! I find that He is using me in new ways out of the changes in my heart.

Pastor, instead of getting into a biblical dissertation I think I would rather answer you in spirit.

Our sexuality is a very significant aspect of who we are and how we live. It is extremely complicated and for many people is a HUGE challenge to manage, to embrace, and to sort out. I want to continue to learn how to grasp the reality of God's movement in us, and through us concerning our sexuality. To simply say, "homosexuality is sin" would be a gross over simplification of a human experience. I also see that even the word homosexuality is truly indefinable as it doesn't really have a meaning that applies to someone's life. What is homosexuality? Is it an erotic attraction, is it emotional desire? Is it a behavior, or an identity? Is it an intrinsic part of our being, or is it a temporary act under the influence of alcohol?

I fully recognize there are created designs, desires, and plans that God has for each of us as His beloved creation. The real dilemma is that each and every day we struggle to find Him in the midst of our humanity and how to reflect His glory to others. I know many incredible people who try desperately to sort out their homosexuality while they also seek to love Jesus with their whole heart.

I also realize that there are Biblical standards that seem to be communicated from God's heart to ours through His word. But under the canopy of the standards, there is a human life experience which struggles to fit into a prescribed box that humanly cannot be explained sometimes. I see these as uniquely different and yet connected deeply to our faith and desire to please a Holy God.

I believe we can all agree that indiscriminate sexual sport is undeniably wrong. However having homosexual attractions and desires for personal connection or intimacy is not something I would call iniquity and therefore I do not believe it is something that would disqualify someone from a growing relationship with Jesus Christ. What one chooses to do with those desires must ultimately be sorted out with Jesus.

Picture with me if you will a ball of yarn that is colorfully variegated. As we experience life with the Lord I see it like the yarn is pulled off of the ball a little at a time.

As it is rolled off it is explored, healed, changed, and moved on. As life unfolds in Christ, there will be many surprises! God is a God of order and will not a bruised reed break. This tells me that He enters our life to sanctify it, but in order and over time. Sometimes, large things are dealt with; other changes can be smaller and incremental. The issues we bring to the table of our growing process in the Lord may be somewhere in the middle of the ball and will come through His fingers in the time that is best.

As the yarn is rolled past His fingers, it is knitted into a wonderfully restored, useful, garment. The yarn may still look the same, but it is woven into something more in line with God's plans for us rather than just a ball of yarn with no real purpose.

From the very beginning of time God was busy making something useful out of something that appeared purposeless. He made mankind out of dirt!

> Then the Lord God formed a man from the dust of the
> ground and breathed into his nostrils the breath of life,
> and the man became a living being. Genesis 2:7

If this yarn were all pulled off at once, erratically, we would find a tangled mess on our hands. Sometimes it sounds like Christians believe that God deals with everything all at one time. If so, it would be knotted, scrambled and less able to be used.

I believe God can remove some very big things with expediency. But who am I to say what a big thing is? My heart's desire is to communicate the gentle purposeful, orderly aspects of a loving God. Over a lifetime He is at work transforming His people with precision.

This last week I received an email from a very significant person in my life. This email reveals my heart more effectively than any other way I could say it.

Dear John,

I don't follow FaceBook much, but I had a bit of time yesterday and I noticed your post which led me to your website articles.

I was raised and lived in a cultish religion. I have broken free from that but now I am always skeptical and distrustful of any religion. I am squeamish around Christians of any ilk, or religious dogma for that matter. I have chosen to seek traditional Indian spirituality. It has been a very personal search because it has no religious dogma.

I went to your website to read the whole thing. I was nervous. I do not handle preaching, piousness, or religious judgment very well at all. After having read some of your writing I have to say that I'm greatly impressed with your insight in regards to the Gay/Christian issue.

When I read what you have written, I realized that there is a possibility that Christians really can be 'Christian' towards others. Until now, I don't believe I have met one that is like that.

But your writing also makes me more hopeful. Thank you for sharing in your life stories that you have written on your website what must have been a horrible experience for you. I had some as well, while not with a family member, and not as a child, my experiences have certainly changed me forever.

My own painful experiences have taken away dreams, beliefs and trust; and in their place they have left me with fear, cynicism, anger, and many wounds. My experience with those in the cult I was with was just as damaging. It left even deeper wounds for me than sexual injury; it left my soul scarred for life.

It was a breath of fresh air to read your piece and hear compassion, a non-judgmental approach. You have given the opportunity for others to think for themselves and act like the Christians they profess to be.

Thank you, John. Not only for your story, but for being a respectful voice in a din of noisy, cackling religious zealots.

Your Friend

Pastor, This letter frames for me the very reason for the ministry approach I have adopted of late. It is my greatest desire to reach out to those who are hurting, scarred, and fearful of traditionally accepted church practice or religion. I desire more than anything to be a bridge to Jesus that is honest, strong, and trustworthy. As I reflect on the ministry vision that we have developed through Grace Rivers I think my heart is very clear.

> Grace Rivers is a ministry with the gay community that reveals the message of an authentic relationship with Jesus Christ and genuine community with His followers because every person deserves to know that Jesus loves them.

Each one of us has a different positional call within our Christian family. Some may be called to proclaim a truth, others called to walk alongside in the truth. I believe I am called to walk alongside.

It is my hope that my own personal mission statement will continue to bear fruit. It is my desire to help people be the very best they can be, and this I know is only through Jesus Christ.

If someone is fearfully estranged from a loving God then, I want to be the loving voice that says, "It will be ok. He loves you. You can trust Him." This is with the hope that they will seek Him all the more themselves.

The teachers of the law and the Pharisees brought in a woman caught in adultery. They made her stand before the group and said to Jesus, "Teacher, this woman was caught in the act of adultery."

"In the Law Moses commanded us to stone such women. Now what do you say?" They were using this question as a trap, in order to have a basis for accusing him. But Jesus bent down and started to write on the ground with his finger.

When they kept on questioning him, he straightened up and said to them, "Let any one of you who is without sin be the first to throw a stone at her." Again he stooped down and wrote on the ground.

At this, those who heard began to go away one at a time, the older ones first, until only Jesus was left, with the woman still standing there. Jesus straightened up and asked her, "Woman, where are they? Has no one condemned you?" "No one, sir," she said. "Then neither do I condemn you," Jesus declared. "Go now and leave your life of sin." John 8:3-11

Many people have brought this scripture to my attention to help me see that Jesus asked the adulterous woman to leave her life of sin because they are concerned that I may have lost my concern for sin. But, what I see here is that the lady had to be brought to Jesus first. In the right order, He made it clear that He had no condemnation in His heart for her first! He connected to her in a very significant and loving way so as to clear the way for Her to follow Him. I believe the message of leaving her life of sin here is more about turning to a lifestyle of pursuing the Kingdom of God, than it is about behavior modification.

Over and over, Jesus spoke to us about living a kingdom lifestyle. All through the Sermon on the Mount He contrasted the law with our human nature to show us we could never reach perfection on our own. He had come to redeem us and to inspire us to leave the kingdom of this world and join Him in His kingdom. It is clear to me that Jesus was not giving this woman another law to follow, but rather He was asking her to join Him and walk into a better future.

So, if you tell a gay man or a lesbian they are to sin no more this can be a cruel and thoughtless thing to ask. It is thoughtless because of the lack of definition of the word and the potential of a severe misunderstanding of what you mean. This is why it is so very important that we point one another to Christ because He can work in our lives in such beautiful ways to show us what He wants from us. The real message of the woman caught in adultery who meets Jesus face to face is just that _ she met Jesus and He showed her what He wanted her to know.

It is also an example of how human's want to deal with people. The Pharisees wanted to stone her. Hmm. Have we also been Pharisees? Do you think that many within the gay community have faced a crowd of Pharisees in their own lives? Who do they need to connect to? Of course, Jesus! And what do you think Jesus would say to the Pharisee? Well, He asked them to evaluate their own lives of sin.

Years ago a lady that went through one of our programs at Love In Action gave a little talk at the completion of her program. She said:

"John Smid is a Pharisee! Much like the woman caught in adultery, he brought me to the feet of Jesus where I found healing and freedom."

I would never want to be thought of as a Pharisee! But I do want to be a man who has found a loving God and hopes to be a vehicle that will bring others to the feet of the Savior.

In all honesty I do not believe I have deviated from the truth. Rather, I believe truth is a discovery, and I have delighted in finding another facet of God's truth.

I hope we are walking together as the Body, one by one, uniquely with purpose and hope and most of all, a desire to bring the lost, broken, estranged, and hurting folks to the redemption of the soul.

Your Friend,

John

"John, I Still Don't Under-
stand What You Are Saying."

September 2011

I received this question from a long-time friend who had read my recent article "John, You Have Deviated from the Truth."

John,

I still don't understand what you are saying at times. I was involved in extramarital affairs. I lost my marriage and am attempting to start fresh with my sexuality and in my walk with Christ. Could

I have stayed in adultery, without repentance, and still been a faithful Christian? Help me understand this.

Blessings,

Your Friend

Dear Friend,

First of all, many of the principles I will use to answer your question are in articles I have already written about in previous blogs. But please allow me to try to compose an answer to your question.

What I am saying more than anything else is that we are all on a journey of transformation. Some people are what I would call pre-Christian and hopefully they will find Christ's salvation to become real for them. Others have already been enlightened to Christ's gift and have started on their transformation journey. But none of us are on the same timeline, and it is very hard to compare life experiences as it relates to our relationship with Christ. And, we all know, no one has achieved perfection yet. We are all falling short of God's standards.

During Jesus' ministry, he dealt heavily with the Pharisees. He constantly challenged their law-oriented religion. Pharisaical thinking and actions expect people to satisfy the Law Code through good behavior and submission to the law. They attempted to teach that we could gain favor with God by being good obedient sons.

Within the church community many still function as though they can earn God's favor through their good works, their clean living, and they expect others to follow suit. But Jesus told the Pharisees that underneath their polished exteriors was a cauldron of stuff that was clearly wrong and needed to be cleansed. Of course, Jesus was trying to show them their need for His salvation in preparation for His sacrifice for their sin. He was certainly not saying that He expected them to clean it up on their own (see Matthew 23:25-27)

Jesus came to fulfill the law Himself so that we are freed from the eternal consequences of sin. He came to give us freedom from condemnation of the law. In acceptance of His gift, He gave us a new heart. Those with His new heart are growing into the likeness of Christ.

What is a faithful Christian? Is it someone whose behavior is perfect? No, none of us is perfect. But can we be closer to perfect than others? Maybe if we are comparing our outward signs of life. But actually I have known you a long time, and I knew you when you were involved in an adulterous affair. Even in the midst of all of that, you were representative of many wonderful manifestations of your walk with Christ. You revealed the fruit of a man who placed your relationship with Christ as an extreme importance. But during that time, you were struggling with your humanity. I never judged your walk with Christ differently after I found out about your adultery. You are a man who knows Christ deeply. I think we really need to rethink what it means to be a man after God's own heart like our old friend David. Was David a faithful God worshiper? I think we would agree that He was faithful to God even when his relationships were really messed up.

There are many people who would call themselves faithful Christians in arrogance while not being willing to look at their own lives honestly. They exhibit religious pride and practice. And there are many gay people who struggle with deep insecurities about their relationship with God because they love Him so much. How do we judge a faithful Christian.

This is a huge can of worms because of the intrinsic nature of homosexuality. It is very complex. How do we define homosexuality? The word itself is really only good as it describes a collection of related items. It is vital to separate behavior from the person. Gay people hear all the time that they must repent of homosexuality. A person cannot repent of homosexuality if the understanding of the word is same-sex attraction and a unique personal response to gender. For the majority of gay people, their life experience is unchangeable and not something that can be repented of. To say that a gay man or lesbian must repent of their homosexuality will certainly be confusing and challenging.

So it is hard to compare heterosexual adultery with homosexuality, and without clarifying our verbiage and context it can become quite mixed up. If on the transformation journey, God moves a gay man to no longer engage in indiscriminate sexual relations then, we can compare that to what you experienced with adultery. This is something that falls into the category of sanctification. But at the same time, we have to be very careful when judging anyone being a faithful Christian if we are only considering behavior. We all know how flawed our lives are. The most powerful and influential spiritual leaders go home to their own human experiences; and if we were to look only at their human behaviors, they would not satisfy the requirements of a perfect God in and of themselves.

So, why would we place a finer grid onto the gay community than we place on other human experiences? Are gay men or lesbian women under a magnifying glass that we are not willing to subject our lives to?

I recently had a pretty passionate discussion with some men about how many Christians can get so angry about homosexuality. I asked why we have not had such a heavy discussion about things like divorce, or greed. Why is the hammer so heavily aimed at gay people and yet there are so many other things that we ignore? We are either under grace, forgiveness, and God's transformation process in each of our lives, or we are not.

Why would the Christian community not want to see as much grace for the homosexual as we seem to have for those who are divorced, or the greedy? Why do I so often hear such negative responses about allowing God's grace to be poured out on gay people who are so misunderstood by society— and even more so by the church? When Jesus began His public ministry, the things He point out to the new disciples were things like anger, divorce and remarriage, prideful praying and fasting, selfishness, and worry! He pointed out our common temptation for hatred and bitterness toward our enemies. He compared these to the law and revealed to the disciples that they desperately needed a Savior.

Why am I being told I have "deviated from the truth" with this issue and living through cheap grace when the hoarders of worldly goods are sitting in church with their hands lifted high? Shouldn't the homosexual be sitting there too, under God's grace? Well, I certainly understand that grace cost our Savior more than we can imagine, or think. But He freely gave it to us. Some people respond to homosexuals as though they are the lepers of our society. They demand that they repent and even then, celibate homosexuals who say "I am gay" are mocked and rejected just because they are attempting to be honest about their sexuality.

When I was worshiping at a large church, without knowing it, I was barred from ministry within the church, rejected, scorned, and gossiped about. Oh, I never saw or heard it for myself. People didn't come to me personally with that announcement. And it wasn't coming from the pastoral staff, because they continued to embrace me completely. There was a continual encouragement from the staff to offer to do things within the church. But there was the old guard who prevented me from serving within their church. I heard all about it later after I left the church. I was involved in ministry to the gays who were unwelcome at their church. I represented the scourge of our society, and they didn't want anything to do with that.

Someone has to be willing to say to the homosexual, "God loves you intimately. He wants you in His house. He will not give you more than you can handle, and along life's path, you are free, totally free. Do not live under shame and condemnation that Jesus didn't place upon you." Who will be willing to be an ambassador of the gospel of grace for anyone who so desperately needs a deeper connection with God?

So, what would Jesus say to us? How would He minister to the gay community today? I think it is clear. Zaccheus (Luke 19:1-10), the woman at the well (John 4), the woman caught in adultery (John 8:3-11), and the young rich ruler (Luke 18:18-25) are just a few examples, and there are so many others. What I see in His response to the fringe of the culture of the day is that He responded to each one differently and always respectfully. There was not a one size fits all response from Jesus. He understood where each one was at and what the next step of their life would need to be. He was known as a man who would eat with sinners! (Matthew 9:10-13). Jesus' responses to the men and women around him were all unique. In listening to the deepest places of their hearts, He didn't respond the same way to any of them.

Interestingly enough, one of the very first converts after Jesus' death and resurrection was a black eunuch (Acts 8:38-40)! This shows you how much God does not discriminate and how much we do. Without question, the eunuchs of Jesus' day were some of the people who fell under condemnation and criticism, just like the gay people of today do. And we all know what black people have gone through in our recent American history.

> "For God so loved the world that he gave his one and only Son, that whoever believes in him shall not perish but have eternal life. For God did not send his Son into the world to condemn the world, but to save the world through him. Whoever believes in him is not condemned, but whoever does not believe stands condemned already because he has not believed in the name of God's one and only Son" (John 3:16-18, NIV).

Sorry if this sounds a little strong. It isn't about you. You just provided a question for me to flush out some more things.

I really appreciate your asking, my friend. I am open to questions and thoughts.

John

Who Did Jesus Invite to His Table?

October 2011

I have been passionate about the Christian celebration of The Lord's Supper as has been taught through an annual Passover Seder. This full length fellowship meal has been a hinge pin of my faith for many years. During our recent trip to England, we attended a retreat where a minister from Scotland taught a message about communion before we celebrated the elements together.

His message got me thinking again about how many people wrestle with their hearts during a typical communion time at church. Originally meant to be a reminder of the Passover, and in Christ, a message of the gospel of freedom, far too many people feel uninvited to partake even though they may eat anyway.

A retreat where there were many gay men and women who are Christians were attending, the minister shared his heart and invited them to partake. He passed around a large loaf of bread and encouraged us to take a piece that would compare to our understanding of God's love for us. He talked about how often people will take a tiny crumb while Jesus promises He will provide enough for all to take.

Tears began to flow from both the wounds of rejection and the gratitude of inclusion while the elements were taken. My heart was grieved when I pondered how many people are hurting and how much Jesus wants them to be embraced.

Communion is an element that is commonly shared throughout the world as a symbol of our faith. Sadly, it is also something that can keep us separated in disunity as well.

When I was a young boy, I remember sitting on the aisle of the long pew at church while people walked forward for communion. In order to maintain my composure of remaining quiet, I looked at all of the shoes. High heels of many colors, shapes, and sizes mixed in with large, black, men's shoes, kept my mind busy while I reverently looked down as though I was praying. Well, that's what I was told to do.

One of the most central sacraments to our Christian faith is Communion. What is it? Where does it fit within our Christian experience, doctrine, and belief? What do we know about it? How have our experiences with this sacrament, shared by those all around the globe, shaped our Christian walk? There are numerous teachings about how to take communion, where to take communion, and who should take communion. What have we learned about ourselves, others, and the church through this symbolic expression?

As I got to the right age as a young Catholic, I was taught about the miraculous transformation of the host and the cup mysteriously into the body and blood of Christ. It was kind of like other mysteries in life, such as Santa Claus and the Tooth Fairy! I just accepted it as something I would never truly understand but the nuns and priests prepared us for the amazing day where we would walk through a rite of passage to our First Communion.

After we had practiced our walk in the church sanctuary many times, we were finally ready for the real thing. We got all dressed up in our suits and ties, the girls in their frilly lace dresses, white gloves, and shiny patent leather shoes. All together in our pews lined up as we had planned, we could now walk up the aisle like all of those ladies and men had done every Sunday. It was an exciting time, and we all perceived we had reached a great new phase in our lives. It was like a rite of passage.

At that very young age communion was not much more than part of the church service, but I'll never forget the taste of the wafer thin host as it entered my mouth. It was kind of like the breath fresheners today as they melt in between your tongue and the roof of your mouth. They called it bread, but it resembled something quite different from bread to me. It was far too thin to call it bread. I was told that the nuns made it and couldn't imagine how they could possibly make these little dime sized paper thin wafers by the hundreds in preparation for each Sunday.

I can't say that taking communion was a spiritual experience for me throughout my childhood, but I faithfully partook each Sunday, since my dad made sure we were there every week. One thing I did think about was that it seemed to be a privilege since it seemed we had to qualify in order to take it. There was the initial series of teachings and what seemed to be a graduation for our First Communion.

Then, there were ongoing qualifiers, such as we had to go to confession to make sure our sins were forgiven. We also couldn't eat before church because there had to be an hour of fasting before taking communion. It seemed that Jesus needed a clean stomach before his body and blood entered into it. At the time, I think I clearly understood His not wanting to mush around in my breakfast remnants.

How did this play a role in my foundation of understanding communion? Well, I can say that it led me to believe that communion was not for the common man, but rather only certain people could walk up that aisle. They had to pass a test, be reverent, clear their consciences, clean their stomachs, and beat their fists against their chests three times when the bells rang before they could follow the plan to "Take, eat, this is My body." There were so many rituals surrounding this mysterious event during the Sunday Mass.

I grew to think of communion as nothing more than a ritual, a rite and something that seemed to be an integral part of the Christian life. But later on as my church associations changed, my thoughts of communion also changed. When I went to a new kind of church it seemed they had different kind of communion. The shape changed! The cup changed. Now they had you stay in your pew and the ushers passed the plates around for each person. We now had designed a little Chiclet shaped piece of bread and a thimble sized cup. It just wasn't the same as being personally served and the wafer melting in my mouth that the Catholic experience held for me. The little cup was different too. As a Catholic, I never tasted the cup. The Priest dunked the wafer into the wine when I was little.

The Pastor would stand up front before the ushers passed around the plates. He would typically charge us with clearing our consciences. During some church services I had experienced. it also seemed that some people who may have been sitting with us were told they might consider not eating with us if they were in trouble with God, or others. There was often beautiful music playing during the passing of the plates; and as I looked around it seemed everyone was in deep prayer, or pretending to be, while they waited for the entire congregation to be served.

There were times when I wondered if maybe I shouldn't take communion. I mean, there were many times when I didn't feel as though I was in a great spiritual place, or that something had been going wrong in my life. But, oh, my gosh, what would people around me think if they noticed I hadn't taken communion? They would know that I was in a bad space and think awful thoughts about my life. I know because one time I noticed someone next to me didn't partake, and I wondered what was wrong with that person. What could be so awful that you wouldn't take communion? Then I had another thought; they must have been spiritual giants in order to go against the flow and actually do like the pastor said: do not eat if we had something wrong in our lives. At least they were honest enough to evaluate their lives deeply. So, I tried to stop judging them and think of them in a better light.

The ritual of communion continued throughout my many years of Christian experience and my walk of faith. I really never thought of the fear and intimidation that often went alongside the Communion Table until I evaluated communion all together. This was until I had my first Passover Seder experience.

I have found that many Christians don't know what a Passover Seder is. I didn't know until I went to my first one. It was at this special event that I learned where communion came from. I learned that when Jesus spoke of eating His body, and drinking His blood, He was speaking at a Passover meal with His disciples. This sheds a whole new light on the bread and the cup! I now saw that it was actually a full meal where He talked about bread and wine.

Later on, I was involved in hosting a Passover Seder. I invited an older woman to the special event. I explained that the Passover Seder had now become one of my favorite holidays each year. She looked at me and said, "What is a Passover Seder?" Much to my surprise since this lady had been a Christian for fifty years. I explained that it was a glorified communion service. She thought for a minute and responded to my invitation. "Oh, John, I'll have to ask my pastor if I can come. He says we aren't supposed to take communion at any other church than our own." She then asked if I was ordained as a minister since she was also taught that only ordained men are to serve communion.

I was shocked at what she had said because it sounded so strange to me. She had been taught that there was something so religious about communion that she actually felt fearful about coming to the Seder without her pastor's permission! Much to her relief, her pastor gave her permission to attend the Seder.

Wow, this led me to do further thinking about this whole communion thing. I realized that for many Christians, fear was tightly woven into the communion experience. The very symbol of the death and resurrection of Christ and the freedom He bought for us had turned into bondage for so many followers of Christ.

Fear of disapproval, fear of failure, fear of breaking a Christian rule or just fear of a disapproving God! From my Catholic roots to protestant teaching, it seemed most often Christians were taught that taking communion had all kinds of rules surrounding it. Where did this come from?

In chapter 12 of Exodus, there are many regulations regarding celebrating the Passover during the Old Testament times. Everything from a perfect lamb to expunging the household of leavened bread, Moses and Aaron received their instruction from the Lord about the celebration festivities. I am sure that most Christians have experienced the fear of taking communion irreverently.

When Jesus was leading the Passover Seder with His disciples, the following gives a recounting of the experience.

> "While they were eating, Jesus took bread, gave thanks and broke it, and gave it to his disciples, saying, "Take and eat; this is my body. Then he took the cup, gave thanks and offered it to them, saying, "Drink from it, all of you This is my blood of the covenant, which is poured out for many for the forgiveness of sins."(Matthew 26: 26)

Certainly many of the historical rules were rooted in the Old Testament experience. The Law has continued to impact many of our lives and our Christian experiences. But when Jesus came, EVERYTHING changed! He brought radical challenges to the Pharisees and the culture of the day in which he lived.

I wonder what it was like for the new disciples of Jesus to take part in the bread and wine this time. At the time I am certain they worked through all of the rituals that were in place for the Jews at the time. But I wonder how the conversation went around the table with Jesus present? Was it stuffy and filled with ritual, or did Jesus bring a flavor of His love and grace even before His New Covenant took place? Oh, yes, He brought forth the reality of the betrayer sitting there which I am sure brought a somber reflection to the table, but certainly the disciples saw something different from the usual Seder.

Now, today, 2000 years later, after instruction is given, we read a selection of passages from First Corinthians chapter 11.

> "This is my body, which is for you; do this in remembrance of me." In the same way, after supper he took the cup, saying, "This cup is the new covenant in my blood; do this, whenever you drink it, in remembrance of me. For whenever you eat this bread and drink this cup, you proclaim the Lord's death until he comes." (1 Cor. 11:24-26)

Often the pastor will lead his congregation to an evaluation that seems to be somewhat ambiguous, but, nonetheless, we are to dig into our heart and souls prior to taking the bread. As I read through the chapter where this practice of evaluation comes from, I see this preface from Paul:

> "In the following directives I have no praise for you, for your meetings do more harm than good. In the first place, I hear that when you come together as a church, there are divisions among you, and to some extent I believe it. No doubt there have to be differences among you to show which of you have God's approval. When you come together, is it not the Lord's Supper you eat?" (1 Cor. 11:17-19)

It seems the major problem Paul is calling us to evaluate is that as a Church, we struggle greatly with division, fighting among ourselves. He even points out that many of our times together do more harm than they do good! He says that the divisions are often rooted in pride about who has God's approval and who doesn't.

This is very important to consider!

What are we called to evaluate before taking communion? It looks as though Paul is calling our attention to the arrogance of judging whether or not someone is good enough to eat with us. I want to point out right here that it is called. The Lord's supper. It is at His invitation that we are partaking. It is His dining table, not ours. Who should be the judge for the invitation? If we think we can be that judge. Then we ourselves are crossing over the very directive that Paul is laying out for us.

As I look back at many of my experiences in preparation for communion, it seems there is a lot inferred about who should or who should not partake. My older friend experienced an extreme example of her pastor leading her to believe that permission must be granted from him for eating the bread and taking the cup at the Seder celebration. I feel grieved that this godly woman had been so misled so as to believe she had to fear sharing in something like a Seder. The fears that often underlie communion experiences are attached to a man's approval of God's invitation. It can seem as though God invites, but man approves.

One time when I was visiting my dad in Las Vegas, I decided I wanted to go to church with him to show him how much I respected his commitment to his faith. I had not been to church with him since I last regularly attended a Catholic mass when I was a teenager and I was digging deep into my heart to attend with him. As the service proceeded towards communion, my dad handed me a folded open booklet turned to the page on communion. It read:

"While we are praying for the unity of the Body of Christ to be revealed, at this time if you are not fulfilling the requirements of a faithful Catholic, we respectfully ask you to abstain from taking communion with us."

I was very upset by what I read. While I understood the intent due to my experience with Catholicism, I also knew the desire of Christ to see his Body come together and to quit separating on denominational lines. When my dad and I got home and I was standing in the kitchen, I opened my heart to him. "Dad, I am very upset by what I read today. While I deeply respect your commitment to the leadership of your church, I want to say that my attending church today was an answer to the prayers that were mentioned in that booklet. I had put aside my flavor of church to attend with you for your flavor of church. I feel very frustrated by the rejection of my heart based on rules that are not based on the gospel. I am a follower of Christ, and you are a follower of Christ. We should be able to share communion together based on our common faith even though there are differences in the way we practice it."

My dad responded, "John, I know what you are saying but that is the way my church is and I felt I needed to honor the wishes of our leadership." I felt comforted that my dad understood what I was saying, yet I still felt frustrated by the separation of Christians bringing disunity to the heart of Jesus to see his kids all together.

Several years ago I asked a second question. If the scriptures said "So then, my brothers, when you come together to eat, wait for each other. If anyone is hungry, he should eat at home, so that when you meet together it may not result in judgment". (1 Cor. 11:33-34)

Then how are we defining communion? If it is possible to overeat at communion, then how does a Chiclet and a thimble full of grape juice relate to communion? There is something here that really needs to be considered.

If a traditional communion is symbolic, I understand the small elements. But in its symbolism, what does it stand for? Well, first of all, it certainly is a symbol of that first historic Passover. I get that part. The symbol of the real night of the Passover is significant, and God has called us to remember this special event in our history.

But, the elements are also symbolic. They are symbolic of the entire meal of the Passover Seder. The original Seder is a time of sharing history, our faith, and certainly friends and family. It symbolizes the entire picture of God's heart for relationship.

Certainly we cannot over eat the elements unless we raid the back store of Chiclet bread pieces and gallons of grape juice. But if the warning is about not being a pig when we go to a fellow's home for dinner, then we need to take a look at our gluttonous practices as we partake of the symbol of communion.

But, it is also symbolic of sharing meals together with other Christ Followers. As I think of my Christian walk, some of the fondest memories I have are eating, drinking, laughing and learning together over a meal. I also recognize that to eat with other Christians with whom I experience unsettled relationships is certainly making light of the unity called for in the Body of Christ. To sit at the vulnerable place of sharing a meal together and put on a facade of unity is a breach of the kind of relationship that God is calling us to celebrate through communion.

But there is something very important to consider here as well. Who is God inviting to the table? Not, who do we want at the table, but who does God want at the table.

Is anyone unworthy to be at the table? Are there those to whom we can say, "Go away until you get your act together!" Maybe we are talking to ourselves. Paul seems to warn us of our divisive ways. Can a pastor or other spiritual leader tell us where, when, and with whom we can celebrate God's Passover elements?

I was recently with a group of gay men and women who were celebrating God's presence. We were led to a time of communion where the leader bought to our minds that any are welcome to the table who desire to draw near to Christ to share in His blood sacrifice bringing us hope, renewal, and eternity.

Behind me was a middle aged man who broke out and wept loudly. His heart was filled with a sense of loss, and yet a sense of inclusion. He later described that because of his being gay, he had always taken communion with a deep sense of guilt and shame and at times even avoided it. He perceived that he was not welcome to the Table of the Lord because of what he had heard others preach about who was worthy to partake and who wasn't.

My heart broke for his experience. I looked back over all of the years of my own experience with communion, and I can see why this man felt uninvited to the Lord's table. It may have been because he wasn't reading the invitation correctly. It was sent by Jesus! It didn't have man's return address on it.

Jesus invites us to His table, anyone who wants to come, can come. Are we passing on the Lord's invitation, or are we making it our invitation? The point I am attempting to make here is that there are Christians who think they can edit the guest list for those invited to the Lord's Supper when it isn't their guest list!

> "While they were eating, Jesus took bread, gave thanks and broke it, and gave it to his disciples, saying, "Take and eat; this is my body."

> "Then he took the cup, gave thanks and offered it to them, saying, "Drink from it, all of you This is my blood of the covenant, which is poured out for many for the forgiveness of sins."

It is the cup of forgiveness for all mankind. Man; woman; black or white; and , yes, lesbian, gay transsexual, or straight.

At the close of the service, the man who led us through communion said something profound:

"When you make homosexuality a fundamental aspect our faith and it divides us into disunity, you are adding to the gospel."

Much like other social issues, homosexuality has seemed to divide our family into segments. There is certainly different schools of thought, practice, and biblical interpretation within the Body of Christ. Sadly, those that suffer from the disagreement are those whom are cast aside, those who perceive they are second class Christians because they are gay. Does the gospel discriminate based on sexual attractions? I believe Jesus in the Bible says all are welcome.

Might we ponder this question? What other things in our Christian communities and personal walk that we make fundamental keep us or others from The Lord's Table that He has invited us to?

Might I say… If we cannot RUN to the communion table with no fears, no hesitation, with full confidence, then where can we run to?

> You foolish Galatians! Who has bewitched you? Before your very eyes Jesus Christ was clearly portrayed as crucified. I would like to learn just one thing from you: Did you receive the Spirit by observing the law, or by believing what you heard? Are you so foolish? After beginning with the Spirit, are you now trying to attain your goal by human effort? (Gal. 3:1-3)

PART TWO

I Acknowledge

In March of 2010, five years after that fateful day in June 2005, I wrote a general apology and sent it to an online news forum called ex-gay Watch. The changes that occurred in my life now brought me to do a thorough evaluation of the years I had labored in ministry. I compiled and published a general public apology in response to some soul searching I had been going through. I have called this series of six topics *I Acknowledge*.

I was in public ministry internationally. I had spoken, taught, and ministered to hundreds, if not thousands, through the years to men and women who are gay or have deeply wrestled with homosexuality. It is due to that very public nature of the sphere of my influence that I feel it is important to very publicly acknowledge the things that I can take responsibility for.

I have decided to attempt to put into words a more detailed communication of those things that are most significant for me to acknowledge. I have been wrong and have made mistakes that I feel I must take responsibility for. It is my goal to write out a separate document for each item that will explain my heart and personal evaluation on these things.

About the Message of Change - Part 1

Through my overt and covert alignment with the presumed message of change through the ex-gay movement, I want to acknowledge that I have communicated through teaching, private conversation and public venues that someone who is gay is less than someone created in God's image. I acknowledge that I was a covert messenger of the false hope for a change in sexual orientation from gay to straight. I perpetuated a message that gave the perception that if someone tried hard enough they would experience a new heterosexual desire that would replace their same-sex desires. Please allow me to explain further why I have come to this conclusion.

> If we claim that we're free of sin, we're only fooling ourselves. A claim like that is errant nonsense. On the other hand, if we admit our sins—make a clean breast of them—God won't let us down; He will be true to Himself. He'll forgive our sins and purge us of all wrongdoing. If we claim that we've never sinned, we out-and-out contradict God, making a liar of Him. A claim like that only shows our ignorance of God (1 John 1:8-10, The Message.)

I want to set the stage in a way that I think will frame this for you. I believe the ex-gay movement began as a connecting point for individuals who desired to reach people within the gay community with the love of Jesus Christ. Fairly quickly, individuals within the founding members began to hope that God had the desire, and the power, to deliver them from homosexuality, which for many included the hope they might be able to became straight.

As they visualized their desires, some grabbed onto this idea in such a way that it became the central message of the ex-gay movement. The ex-gay movement in association with the faith doctrine that became prominent in the 1970s (meaning if we claim it in Jesus' name, He will bring it to pass if we have the faith to believe it will occur) began to proclaim change through Jesus Christ. This concept of change also became extremely ambiguous and was defined differently by each individual but was maintained as a very generic statement.

Now since the early seventies men and women throughout the world have sought God for change that they hoped would include a change in orientation from homosexual to straight. They believed this could occur through faith in Jesus, prayer, counseling, changes in sexual behavior, and obedience to God.

This intimate desperation was often fueled by an inner belief that as gay men and women, they were intrinsically flawed, broken, damaged goods, and certainly less than God's best. The desire to change came with the hope that somehow a transformation from gay to straight might allow for an upgrade on God's list of approved people. If straight people were better, more loved and closer to God, then people who are gay would do anything they could to achieve this change.

So, ex-gay ministries began to sail on the faith-filled hope of those that came to them with the desire for intrinsic changes in their sexual desires. In some ministries, unorthodox counseling and prayer practices were used to manipulate more hope for change. Most often these strange actions were quick to go away. But the faith in change from gay to straight continued. Though it was not always spoken boldly, many remained hopeful they would see it happen for themselves.

Christian communities and churches also loved the message of change for people who were gay. Certainly many of them were motivated to help their friends. But for some who didn't really cherish the thought of embracing gay people into their church, they hoped if they could become straight it would take away the difficulty of having to deal with homosexuality.

Parents became a strong thread through this movement. Their prayers were fervent; deeply seated in pain, confusion and for many, embarrassment. There were even some parents who believed as long as their children were gay, they could never make it into God's eternal resting place. I heard a mother tell me in a group meeting, "You mean I can pray for my son's salvation? I thought all gays were an abomination and had no hope for eternal life with Jesus."

Christian parents and their heartfelt desire to see their gay loved ones relieved of the burden of homosexuality became the backbone of many ministries around the country. Parents became invested in the message of change through God's amazing power to do anything if they prayed and believed. They hoped that God would change their loved ones' homosexual orientation.

When I was a new Christian, a friend invited me to an event where the minister promised deliverance to those involved in homosexuality. I girded up my heart and attended the event, but I didn't get my miracle. I saw no change in my sexual desires, and my hope quickly turned to disappointment and depression.

A year or so later, I discovered ex-gay ministries. I got the opportunity to become a staff member for a nationally known ministry, Love In Action. Upon my arrival, I found leaders, churches, and individuals who held tightly to the message of change. The leader, Frank Worthen, was in fact himself married to a woman. That certainly appeared to be a model of change to strive for.

We spoke of change often. We prayed for deliverance, and worked through teaching material that was described as *Steps Out of Homosexuality*. All of the terminology, the structures, and the conversations centered around the hope that at some point, somehow, God would set us free from what was described as the bondage of homosexuality.

I became deeply invested in the hope that God would set people free and began to answer phone calls, counsel men and women, and later became the Director for the ministry that proclaimed freedom for the homosexual. I did find freedom from unhealthy relationships and patterns of manipulation and sexual promiscuity. I praise God for what He has done, but still I found no change in orientation.

Along the way, I attended conferences, went through some of my own private counseling, prayed, studied and read books that all promised that I would eventually find the freedom I was looking for. In faith, I believed it would come true, and therefore I offered others the same message for their own lives.

We stood together as brothers along the road. We believed it was absolutely necessary to have a good support team who agreed with us and walked the path alongside us. It was clear that we could not allow any messages from the outside to infiltrate our minds so as to thwart our hope for what we believed God was going to do. I clung to the belief and hope that over time, I would eventually see more internal changes.

Along the way I struggled with my own internal thoughts, attractions and desires. I believed it would be wrong to talk about them and fearful that if I did, I would somehow ruin the testimony that God was creating within me. I didn't hear of anyone else who was talking about their own remaining attractions—well, at least not among the leadership. I thought surely they had found what I was hoping for, so it was important to continue pressing on.

There were group members and people who would call us talking about their attractions. But our job was to build up their faith that God could, and would, change all of that if they believed He could, and would. It was important that they also did the right things to obey God along the way.

One night I dreamed that I was in a large Gothic cathedral. A very strange female preacher was pointing her finger at the congregation saying loudly, "You're gay! Admit it, you're gay!" I was sitting with some friends and immediately I stood in defiance and said, "I will not sit here and listen to this." My friends said, "John, sit down, you need to hear everything she is saying."

When I awoke the next morning, life was different. I seemed to gain the conviction through this dream that I had to be honest about what I was feeling inside regardless of what others would say about my honesty. The preacher was right—I remained attracted to men as I always had been. Prior to that dream, I was adamant not to be honest. From that time forward I continued to talk freely and honestly about what change was for me, and what it wasn't. But the overarching message of the ministry and the entire ex-gay movement continued to covertly say, "You can change." In my mind I was no longer dishonest about my own same sex attraction, yet I didn't realize the many ways I was still a representative of a faulty message that was giving a false hope for a change in sexual orientation.

That year, 1995, I gave a plenary session talk at the national Exodus conference titled *Honesty, Is It the Best Policy?* It was in this talk that I revealed to the entire audience that I was still experiencing homosexual attractions and challenged the listeners to a deeper level of honesty. My talk angered some but thankfully, it gave hope to many others. One young lady from Australia stepped up to me afterwards and said, "John, thank you so much for your authenticity. Last night I had almost given up hope on God and myself. But today, I have a renewed belief that God loves me and I can continue." Well, I guess being honest was a good thing! I was also motivated to continue to be honest.

As I look back over all that time, I regret the years of my own dishonesty. I acknowledge that through my own weakness I was fearful of stepping out and becoming more honest that change of sexual orientation, barring a miracle of God, was not a reality for most people. I failed to recognize the duplicitous message within our communication. "You can change, but I haven't" was something, I am sorry, but I didn't see coming out of our ministry.

At Love In Action, we leased a billboard with a giant picture of me on it. We had it for one year in central Memphis near the gay community. With great pride I had my picture on top of a huge building with the words which read:

"I Used To Be a Homosexual" (1 Cor. 6:9-11)

There was literally no response from the display. No one came to our ministry running to find freedom because they saw my giant picture and those verses referenced. I've thought about that many times since, and I realized it was deceptive! I didn't used to be a homosexual. I was still a homosexual! And to proclaim something that was untrue was something that I don't believe God could bless. It was dishonest.

I also must be clear that sexual desires fall on a continuum. For some who experience same-gender attractions, they may also experience satisfying sexual attractions to those of the opposite sex. I do not consider this change. Rather it is a result of the uniqueness in human sexuality. It is commonly called bisexuality. It is very hard to place people into a box regarding their sexual attractions and behaviors.

The teachings of the ex-gay movement often opened the door for some to believe that one who is gay is less valuable to God and less loved by Him as they are. Therefore change was seen as desirable, and for some, necessary. It is easy to understand that if there is so much emphasis on change, then it is easy for someone to believe that God would be happier with them if they were straight.

I want you to know that if you are gay, you are loved by God as you are. The homosexual orientation is no one's choice and it does not in any way take away from God's desire to know you, love you, and save you from an eternity without Him. Everyone is born intrinsically flawed and in need of God's redemption through Christ. No one is any farther away from God than another and all are equally able to seek Jesus for the salvation of their lives.

"So don't sit around on your hands! No more dragging your feet! Clear the path for long-distance runners so no one will trip and fall, so no one will step in a hole and sprain an ankle. Help each other out. And run for it! Work at getting along with each other and with God. Otherwise you'll never get so much as a glimpse of God. Make sure no one gets left out of God's generosity. Keep a sharp eye out for weeds of bitter discontent" (Hebrews 12:12-15, The Message).

Addictive Sexuality? - Part 2

Through the ministry of Love In Action I worked to develop an addiction, twelve step approach with the mindset that we were helping men and women to recover from homosexuality. With that model we began to teach that homosexuality, same-sex attractions and behaviors, were addictions. I taught that homosexual attractions were a result of unhealthy and unresolved feelings from childhood wounds. Subsequently, I believed that if healing could occur for those wounds, it would take the power out of the homosexual compulsions and allow someone to live free from homosexuality.

I acknowledge that we wrongly applied therapeutic tools and structures that were designed to help people who were facing chemical dependencies and sexual addiction, but were never designed for use with homosexuality.

I have learned how an addiction model makes the assumption that people who are gay need recovery. This mindset can produce confusion, shame, guilt, and can perpetuate the faulty message that gay people are damaged goods and deceived. I am now aware of how this conflicts with what God is trying to say to His children about who they are in Him, loved and adored as His sons and daughters.

I acknowledge that this program model was woefully misguided. This model paid little attention to what a person was truly experiencing. We as the staff held to a "we know better" reaction to their lives. I also acknowledge there was harm done and pain inflicted due to using the wrong model and wrong tools. We often had closed ears to hear the hearts of those we said we loved.

How did this come about? In 1995 Love In Action began a new season of ministry after moving to Memphis. In the previous years we had been focused on a relational approach with a Christian teaching and community-based ministry model. The ministry was more of a discipleship program with some special teaching about the origins of homosexuality and Christian principles to learn to live obediently in Christ. As the Director I was constantly evaluating the outcome of our effort. I honestly could see that there was great room for improvement since the evidence was stacked against us that not many had experienced real change from a homosexual orientation. I believe the men and women who came to us often received encouragement and in some cases changed lives and improved relationships.

When we began to settle into Memphis, we were introduced to another ministry that was deemed the cream of the crop in treatment for adolescents with chemical dependencies. Their track record was noted as one of the most successful in the country. We were invited to sit in on their ministry groups and staff meetings. So for many weeks and months, our staff rotated in and out of their groups and believed that what we were seeing was solid and provided changes. But as I look back, honestly, I saw a legalistic approach and disrespectful communication from the staff to the clients.

It was very uncomfortable at times to hear the exchanges, but actually most of our staff were swept into the successful reputation and didn't really look at the harm being done in many cases. As I looked at the lack of success we had experienced previous to our move, I hoped to find something that might work better. They seemed so confident in their work and were very well supported.

Also around this time, Exodus International leaders had begun to discuss the importance of becoming more main stream within the professional counseling realm. The ministry with the addiction model utilized trained, and licensed counselors, so it seemed to be just the ticket to help us move forward. I believed they would certainly know better than we did how to do this!

I was taught about dual relationships within the counseling field being harmful for recovery and counselor/client relationships. So it seemed we had been doing it all wrong and would never be recognized as a professional organization in counseling networks. Our staff and counselors had previously been very relationally connected to our clients. Within a few months I made a knee-jerk decision to change virtually everything we had in place. The counseling director was shocked at our previous practices that were open, honest, and more relational. She made it very clear we were unethical and needed to change what we were doing. I was motivated by what we had been told was harmful to our clients and felt compelled to do whatever it took to do it right.

We decided to implement the model, the tools, the ethics and practices we learned through our time with the other program. It appeared that most of our staff was on board with what we had seen and so we worked hard to change it all around. I thought we were now coming into a whole new level of accomplishment and that we would see much better outcomes and changes in our clients' lives. I also thought we had entered into adulthood in ministry.

The program became more rigid, less relational, and far more clinical. Just as we had hoped, it seemed we were gaining more credibility within the Christian world. We used terms they understood that were common in recovery worlds, such as therapy, client, and counseling practices. This is where we began searching incoming clients for what we called False Images. These were otherwise known as contraband, but we found other terms that seemed to fit what we were doing. We had professional counselors as guides and teachers. Our staff worked on finishing degree programs in counseling and therapy. We had a seasoned and licensed therapeutic counselor as our Clinical Director, so it all felt so legitimate and healthy. It all seemed so positive to us.

Little did I know we were using the wrong methods and tools—and that we had the wrong heart as we related to those in the gay community. We were arrogant, thinking we knew best how to treat those who came to us for understanding and hope. We felt proud that amongst Exodus International circles we had the better approach.

We had our critics as well. Many outsiders, especially family members, really disagreed with our approach. Those who were less knowledge-able than we were had the sensitivity that we were crushing those that came to us with rules and stringent expectations. But we did all we could to explain the value of our program and structures. We were so confi-dent that I think we dominated over them with our words and strength. So, many were silenced just to go along with the program because they wanted so badly for their loved ones to change, to get fixed.

As we researched other addiction programs around the country it appeared we were as good as they were. We had many of the same structures, we now had licensed counselors on staff. We didn't charge nearly as much as they did! Our $6,000 price for three months of resi-dential treatment was certainly a bargain compared to other programs that were charging $20,000! So we had no problem recommending our program and receiving the fees along with it.

All of this was based on the belief that homosexuality is an addiction. Now, some of our clients were truly presenting addictive behaviors. But for those who weren't, we tried to get them to see their value in being part of the accountability needed to keep the structures in place for the real addicts.

People in the Christian community spoke highly of our approach because we seemed so confident we knew all the answers to relieving the burden of homosexuality from their churches, families, and in their own lives. After all, we were Exodus' oldest and most established ministry!

Through this experience I began a teaching that homosexuality was a facade, an ambiguous cover-up for internal issues that remained unresolved. I wrote a lengthy teaching series entitled *The Homosexual Myth*. It was based on the idea that there was no such thing as a homosexual person, rather only actions and behaviors. I taught that each man and women was created as heterosexual but that at some point in their lives they began to experience same-sex attractions. All of these teachings completely minimized the reality of life experience as a gay person. It placed a grid over the life of a man or woman that completely ignored the unique experiences that most gay people have lived.

That set off a firestorm within the gay community against me, against us. They felt invalidated, unheard, and minimized. I felt arrogant about having found the truth about homosexuality. I remember many talks among our staff where we arrogantly believed we had the cutting edge on these issues.

Again, many Christians spoke of how they understood our perspective and how much clarity it gave them to better understand their homosexual loved ones. We tied all of this in to another teaching on Child Development. We held strongly to a developmental model regarding the origin of homosexuality and spoke often that we didn't ascribe to a born homosexual theory. Of course we also gave room for the lack of scientific evidence to the contrary. The Child Development teachings caused a lot of confusion, guilt, unanswered questions and at times created an environment for upsetting families due to searching for the problems that caused the homosexual condition in the first place.

It wasn't until I left Love In Action that I began to evaluate this perspective. I began an effort to reconnect with former Love In Action clients and really tried to open my ears to hear their real feelings. I tried hard to understand their pain, confusion, and overall disappointment in the outcome of their program experiences.

As I listened, I often heard that they felt invalidated. One man looked me right in the face and with passion said, "John, I am NOT an addict!!!" He followed up by explaining that he was never sexually active and how confused he had been in the program since we spoke so often about addiction. It just didn't apply to his life at all! But we held to the theories that even his attractions fit our addiction model, which of course didn't resonate with his kind and sensitive heart.

Other folks I talked with spoke of how hard it was to connect with God on an intimate level when there was so much emphasis on how their hearts were deceitful and wicked. We referred to that Old Testament passage in relationship to our human experience. They said it was so hard to trust themselves, their own life experience, feelings, and other factors when we taught they were always going to be evil and deceived.

There were some who thrived in the addiction model because they were clearly struggling with addictive behaviors. These folks found deep levels of freedom from the compulsions they suffered. Of course, because it was a helpful model to deal with addiction! But the problem was confusing the issues. Were they dealing with addiction, or homosexuality, as the presenting issue? When they were combined, then they saw their humanity as the problem and since their homosexual desires didn't change, then it became a serious spiritual problem in relating to God.

Many others referred to the coldness of the environment at Love In Action. Of course, again, this was after we implemented the addiction model, because there was a time when Love In Action was a loving, connected, relational community. Prior to 1995 there were far fewer complaints about the program and less wounding experienced.

As I write through these realities I feel disappointed in myself. I feel convicted of my wrong ideas and their application that were so wounding for many men and women who, in my heart, I truly wanted to help. I feel embarrassed to admit the depth of my own deception!

For most of my life I have heard that gay men are such sensitive people. Many have known people within the gay community who are caring, loving, and relationship wired. The significance of these truths plays out in why an addiction model is so wounding and harmful.

Often addiction models coincide with traditional intervention models. This is a strong confrontation of the presenting problem, drawing strong boundaries that threaten separation and a loss of connection. When people have personalities that are socially and relationally wired, traditional intervention models can be deeply wounding. The fears of rejection and separation are extremely painful for many if not most gay people when they experience threats from people that they will no longer be with them if they continue in their behavior. The approach based on a threat almost always causes an emotional shut down and prevents a working atmosphere and hopes are lost all around.

Presenting someone who is gay with an intervention model says, "You had better change your homosexuality or else you will lose me." Oh, my, this is an impossible trap! This will never be accomplished; therefore, the relationship with people whom they love the most will be forever lost because they know that they will not likely ever see a change in their homosexuality.

And, of course, I now retract my theories that there is no such thing as a homosexual person. I now believe in intrinsic homosexuality, that many people experience what is virtually unchangeable with the exception of a miracle.

Are you, like me, beginning to feel overwhelmed? Take some time to think through these matters and allow yourself to ponder the goodness of God in a very faulty world. I must do that myself as I evaluate all of these challenging things that I have been responsible for.

Where Does It Come From? - Part 3

I acknowledge that I taught material on child development theories to individuals in our program as well as to groups of parents with a bias towards a developmental causation of homosexuality.

I would often teach that we really didn't know the cause of homosexuality and that science had not found definitive answers to its origins. However, I confused this message through the content of material I taught.

Teaching child development with an overlay of my own life development, I would often relate it to how I believed I had become gay. Since science had not found absolutes, I was arrogant in teaching information as if I knew the origins!

I have always been a person who asked lots of questions about life and experience. Through the years of my own journey I looked for solutions to my own pain and confusion. When I learned about child development theories, I found them to be a great way to seek answers to the deeper questions I had been asking about my childhood experiences. They helped me to grow in greater understanding of myself.

Since I was in an environment for over twenty years that taught that no one was born gay, then I figured there must be answers that could be found in our childhood experiences. So I went on a personal quest to lay out a timeline of my life. I attempted to lay child development theories over the top to help me figure things out.

As I did this, it seemed to make sense to me that I had been born neutral and that things I went through had impacted me to develop same-sex attractions during puberty. So I thought, "This is it!" It was the experiences of my life that merged with my chemistry and bingo —I became gay! I have since changed my perspective on this.

The deeper problem with this material is that it is very easy to place responsibility on the parents and loved ones of a gay person for their homosexuality. It could be assumed then, that if the dad was distant or the mom overly close and too protective, the cause could be found in the developmental process and therefore with the parents! If there was neglect or abuse from a parent or loved one, then the gay person could say it was his or her parents' fault.

As parents and loved ones came to conferences or counseling weekends at Love In Action, and sadly, many other national events, they would come with grave concerns for those they loved. Child development theories were often taught at these events. In their attempts to seek answers that might fix their kids, it was very easy for the grief-stricken parents to take on unhealthy responsibility for something in their child's life that many people would call sin. Therefore, the parents could go away not with freedom, but with greater burdens, that they caused the sin in their child's life.

> "John, my parents came to one of the Love In Action conferences and left with such grief that I don't believe my mom ever got over it. She was concerned about me and said that she felt guilty that she was such a bad parent all of my life. She went to her grave never feeling free from this deep burden."

I think child development theories are a great tool to process a person's life and find some answers. But when attached to homosexuality, they can easily be greatly misinterpreted by many who are listening.

Oh, I always prefaced my teaching with clear communication that I didn't believe a parent caused their child's homosexuality. One of my statements was , "Don't be arrogant—you don't have enough power to create a homosexual child." But all of my warnings could not forestall a parent's sense of responsibility, grief, and desire to repair their child's homosexual inclinations.

I was asked to speak at a parents conference a couple of years ago after I gained insights about the seriousness of this issue. I told the host that I would not be teaching child development at the conference because I believed it could cause harm to those attending.

Since I have become aware of the harmful potential of this material, I have been doing some of my own study regarding the origins of homosexuality. I have had my eyes opened up to some amazing new insights.

I have learned that it is highly possible that many of the things that I used to say caused a homosexual orientation may have in fact been a result of being gay to begin with. Things such as a distant father. Was the father distant because he really didn't understand how to relate to a son who was gay? I think this far more likely.

Or what about an overprotective mother? Was she sensitive to her son because she intuitively knew that he was being teased, ridiculed, and set aside because of this unique gender orientation? Most likely.

Did the dad come very close to the daughter because he sensed she needed the nurturing from him that he felt may help her adjust to being lesbian but just didn't understand what it was all about? Was the mom conflicted with her daughter because she truly couldn't relate to her daughter's perspective on life and relationships? I'm sure this was likely the case.

And is it possible that a dad or mom's history with same-gender relationships created conflicts when they saw a budding gay son, or lesbian daughter? It just may be so.

If I think I have learned anything about all of this, it is that we just don't have all of the answers. Truly, we don't know all the mysteries of our development and their application to our lives. Some answers come over time, but there are so many other questions that remain.

I have attended over 35 Love Won Out conferences all over the country. These were one-day events produced by Focus on the Family. They were typically attended by anywhere from 500 to 1,000 people consisting of mainly parents. They hosted teachings by psychologists who believed in developmental theories, so child development came along with the package. Men and women shared their stories of disconnection with parents in several of the workshops as examples of these theories. Tears of sadness, grief, and an ability to relate flowed from many of those in attendance.

As I stood at my booth, the parents would flood out of the auditorium heading straight towards us with red eyes and Kleenex in their hands. They were full of questions, and I handed out hundreds of copies of our material that they could take with them that would confirm what they had just heard.

I don't think I have ever seen such a large gathering of grieving parents in my life. It was as though they had all lost their children to death and gathered for a common memorial service.

During those years I attended as an exhibitor, I thought I could comfort them by helping them to figure out why their kids were gay. I thought, erroneously, that somehow with my great knowledge of child development, I could help them figure it out.

Instead, what was needed was to help them accept their children as they are and to realize that they really couldn't fix them. I have found that the point at which parents accept their children as being gay is really where authentic relationship begins! The parents find real adult connections that they had longed for, and the children finally feel the love from their parents that they hadn't perceived was there. This is a win/win situation for all concerned.

Thousands of pamphlets went forth, hundreds of parents left knowing they weren't alone. But in the end, nothing got fixed. The grief didn't go away. It may have even gained more power.

Years later, when I have been able to connect with some of these parents, they have said, "Oh, I have come to accept my son (or my daughter) the way he is. We don't always agree, but we have a better relationship than we've ever had. I realized I couldn't fix him. I stopped handing him books, digging for details, and scraping the scabs of our relationship wounds. We've finally found peace. We are all actually much happier and have gone on with life in a better way now."

> "All this is from God, who reconciled us to himself through Christ and gave us the ministry of reconciliation: that God was reconciling the world to himself in Christ, not counting people's sins against them. And he has committed to us the message of reconciliation. We are therefore Christ's ambassadors, as though God were making his appeal through us. We implore you on Christ's behalf: Be reconciled to God. God made him who had no sin to be sin for us, so that in him we might become the righteousness of God" (2 Corinthians 5:18-21).

Love In Action Structure - Part 4

I acknowledge that through Love In Action's teaching and program activities we established structures and rules that clients had to adhere to that promoted traditional gender roles and society's assumptions.

We held our clients accountable regarding how men and women express themselves through their appearance. We also brought exposure to hobbies and activities that were traditionally male or female. Our structure and teaching stifled individuality and authenticity.

When I began to look at this aspect of our program and its ministry focus, I felt defensive and attempted to push back from this critique. I taught sessions on the variety of people, personalities, and expression. I got defensive because I thought certainly I believed that people had to have the freedom to express themselves. I knew there were conservative people, artistic people, uniquely gifted people, and that there was a continuum of style that people utilized to express themselves. I didn't believe I was stifling individuality!

I had one topic I called *Masculinity and Femininity* in which I explored the intrinsic differences between men and women as well as the broader aspect of how culture puts us into boxes that we cannot live in. So I felt confident that I covered this issue in a balanced way.

What I taught and the program structure were at odds with each other. But as I looked at the bigger picture of our ministry, I had not considered the rules and structure of the program that held people to gender stereotypes. Women were led to purses and dresses in their specialized counseling agendas; men were taught masculine experiences like sports and held to short haircuts and no facial hair as part of their programs.

Our motives were to encourage them to try out things that might be challenging, or even scary. In some cases these counseling practices were very effective, but in others they were harmful. I believe we were unable to see the harm when it occurred because underneath there was a cultural stereotype that we hoped would be achieved. It was an underlying goal to neutralize and to move towards a subjection to conservative living in the eyes of the Christian culture.

I have learned that for many gay men and women, forcing a traditional gender expectation can produce tremendous anxiety and bring about even greater shame. Honestly, I understand the anxiety that can come about through forcing these types of things. But I had spent a lot of energy pushing this anxiety away and hid it underneath my own life. I always thought I was an advocate for the men and women who had come to the program but honestly, I wasn't confident in my own experiences and really wasn't what I thought I was.

I remember when Cheryl, who didn't carry a purse and wore very short hair, was taken for a makeover and shopped for her first purse. There was a lot of attention given, and wonderful ladies were very loving through the process with her. They took her shopping, to the nail salon, and affirmed her for the new look. Cheryl loved the attention and was thankful for the relationships. But in the end she was confused, and not welcoming of these new things.

I remember commenting on her purse and her new look, trying to help her see how much more fitting it was to the Christian culture. In the end, she said over and over she was uncomfortable carrying a purse and her hair quickly returned to the shorter style.

I feel sad today that I was so pursuant of her changes, not allowing her to discover her own tastes and believe in her own ability to find what she liked and didn't like. I was more interested in her fitting in than I was finding her own individual expression.

So as I continue to review these things I fully recognize that I had my own divided thinking. I taught one thing, but in the structure of the program another message came through loud and clear: Conform to society! Neutralize your look, your appearance, so that others will be more accepting of you.

We all know that we get some of our most creative geniuses from those in the gay community! Why would we want to stifle them, or corral them into a neutralized box? Art, music, food, décor—we are all blessed by the unique gifts that come from the more creative types. Something else that we often forget, those who are gay are also often those who are more sensitive to relationships, caring, and full of mercy. Stifling their wonderfully and amazingly gifted personalities removes the heart and soul from our communities.

The damage that can occur from attempting to stereotype people into comfortable boxes is very costly to them and brings a huge loss in our own life experience.

Oh, sure, there were men who discovered they loved sports, and women who discovered they loved getting their nails done. People were brought to a place of facing their fears and moved forward. Some people found different careers that were satisfying for them to discover. Moving toward college, or changes in life choices, brought some into improved lives. I know it wasn't all bad.

But what I am feeling responsible for is the lack of freedom for people to discover these things for themselves and to listen more intently to those who didn't find a desire to do so.

A personal life fear of mine has always been team sports. When I was 19 years old I remember vividly talking with a close friend and confiding in him that I didn't like football. I had grown to understand that being male and liking football were synonymous. I felt tremendous anxiety about verbalizing that I didn't like football. Admitting this meant I was uncovering myself and allowing someone to see that I was less masculine due to my dislike of this sport.

I had a huge problem every year when the Super Bowl would come around. It was a time of the year when a tremendous amount of shame would come over my life, and I tried to do the best I could to just numb myself out and stay hidden from others so they wouldn't know I didn't understand the sport, I didn't know who was playing, and certainly didn't watch the game. For me it was like saying I didn't celebrate Christmas!

If someone had pushed me into watching the game I would have felt even more shameful. It seemed that liking football and watching the Superbowl were expected norms of life—and I wasn't normal.

One Superbowl Sunday I was home and my wife was taking a nap. I saw a bunch of men on the balcony across the way loudly cheering and obviously celebrating the holiday of our culture. I felt safely removed from the event and flipped the channels to come across the game. It was the end of the game and the score was very close. I found myself drawn to the competition. In the end I kind of enjoyed the rush of who is going to win? I was not pressured by anyone to watch the game. No one was there to make me feel stupid or ill equipped as a man.

After that event I felt safer the next year and decided to host a Super Bowl party. I found that if I hosted it, I could focus on what I wanted to. We had games, great food, and people could watch, or not watch, the game. It was just a reason to get together. I still don't like football. I never know who's playing, and I don't understand the structure of the sport. I also don't feel so embarrassed to speak this out loud. Liking football, I discovered, is NOT synonymous with being male.

In all honesty, I think some of the reason for these structures and challenges come from my own personal fears. I have never fit into a traditional male form, and probably never will. I've always vacillated from conservative to expressive, trying to find my own personal place in life. I have feared not fitting in if I were to be different, so I conformed. This never really helped me to fit in any better because the issues were more internal than external. I still felt different.

I had a hard time accepting the uniqueness of my own life because I felt less than others, and certainly not like other men. I believed if I could find a more conforming life that I would feel better about myself and not so separated from the stereotype of what our culture deems normal.

My personal struggle was brought into the program that I had established. My own pursuit of overcoming my unique nature and personal compromise in order to gain the affirmation and acceptance of the world around me affected the ministry I led. I feel personally responsible, and grieved that I can now see this.

As I continue to find my natural place in life, I realize I didn't consider the need for others to find their place. Hair styles, colors, career choices, and special interests all play a role in people finding themselves and discovering their unique, God-given nature.

We used to call some of the outward choices False Images and attempted to remove them. I now see that Cheryl's purse was a false image for her and thankfully, she had enough courage to reject the purse because she knew it just didn't fit her. A short hair cut for some men was also a false image for them. False images are those things that are not fitting with the true person inside. Rather than trying to help people find their unique nature, we actually tried to cover it up with what the culture deemed normal.

Today I would encourage people to discover what is real for them, what fits them and is comfortable and natural to their personalities. When I look at modern programs like American Idol I find that I really enjoy the creative appearances of some of the contestants. It is those who are unique and real that I find myself drawn to more than those who are trying to just fit in to win. God made us each unique. This can be uncomfortable for some, but what are the alternatives? The loss of one's soul of life.

> "For you created my inmost being; you knit me together in my mother's womb. I praise you because I am fearfully and wonderfully made; your works are wonderful, I know that full well. My frame was not hidden from you when I was made in the secret place. When I was woven together in the depths of the earth, our eyes saw my unformed body. All the days ordained for me were written in your book before one of them came to be" (Psalm 139:13-16, NIV).

I desire the freedom to continue to discover who I am and how God created me to be. I also want others to find this too!

> "For all of you who were baptized into Christ have clothed yourselves with Christ. There is neither Jew nor Gentile, neither slave nor free, neither male nor female, for you are all one in Christ Jesus. If you belong to Christ, then you are Abraham's seed, and heirs according to the promise" (Galatians 3:27-29, NIV).

The Good, Bad, and the Ugly - Part 5

I acknowledge that through over 20 years of ministry with hundreds of men and women there were many misguided elements that were wounding, confusing, and just plain wrong.

But, I also want to acknowledge that it wasn't all bad. I've received some emails and messages from people who have commented on the good things they received from being a part of Love In Action, or Exodus.

Most of the comments I have received from thankful participants have been focused on gaining courage, learning how to build better relationships, improving on communication skills, and having more confidence. There have been comments on how much better their family relationships are. Some have told me about the growth away from unhealthy and addictive behaviors. Many have spoken about how they have become closer to God and better understand His love for them.

I often joked that I was a part of the long-term program. In over two decades of being involved with Love In Action, I grew to become a more mature and healthy person in general.

But I can also say I was wounded, confused, and held hostage to deceptions and misguided truths. So I want to share the mix of the things that were good and how my own experience with all of this affected me.

I'd like to give some insights as to how all of this affected me personally. When I became a Christian I had failed at three significant gay relationships and I was in a tremendous amount of pain. I needed something greater than my own mess to show me that life could be better. As I discovered a relationship with Jesus I realized He loved me, heard my heart, and was willing to walk alongside me.

One of the first relationship decisions as a new Christian was to seek out a partner that was a Christian. Within a short amount of time, I met a godly, giving, healthy young man. He was an amazingly good influence on me. I was now a Christian, I was out as a gay man, I had good friends and a community that loved me right where I was and included my partner. But nonetheless, after many challenges I was beginning to integrate my life.

In short order, our relationship failed because I was not healthy in my heart or in my ability to be a good steward of an intimate relationship. The internal work on my heart hadn't progressed very far at this point. We walked away from each other, and my life felt so empty that I went back to my old connections. I hooked up with an old partner and returned to the bar scene. The pain rushed back along with the depressive feelings I wanted so much to be gone.

I found an escape valve and left my partner. I walked into a singles ministry and a church that seemed to be a good place to land. And it was in many ways. I was loved by new friends and my mentor/pastor. I was finding a good place to rest that replaced my hunger to return to the unhealthy relationship I had just left. I knew I didn't want all of that to be a part of my life again.

My sexual desires seemed to have waned. The fresh new life seemed to kind of snuff out the sexual drives that had been present. I was comfortable with my new friends for the most part, but underneath I still knew I was gay.

There was little opportunity to talk about being gay other than with a good friend who would listen. But I wasn't totally honest with him because most of our conversations were spiritual in nature and I just didn't lay it all out on the table. He was pretty vulnerable with me and our relationship grew, but I quickly became jealous of his spiritual walk and his heterosexuality.

I became overwhelmed as I struggled in this relationship, which caused some confusion and created barriers to my ongoing growth. I continued to stuff my internal desires in an attempt to be like the others around me. I was very lonely in my heart, but honestly I was relieved to not have to deal with having an intimate relationship like the ones I had with the men previous to becoming a Christian.

So I fully embraced the world of evangelical Christianity. I was taught biblical concepts, I was very active in the church community, and I quickly learned the right and wrong ways to live. It was very clear from all I was taught that homosexuality was a sin. This left me with no options; everything I had buried in my heart had to stay there. I needed to learn how to move on. But move on to what? I didn't know. I only assumed it was a better place because that was what I was told it would be.

I was lonely for intimacy and realized that if a same-sex relationship was out of bounds, then maybe I should try to find a girl again. So, I met a couple of ladies and dated them. Each one ended badly due to unfulfilled desires for everyone concerned. I felt guilty that my initiative in pursuing them caused all of us further harm. I met another lady who seemed interested in something more with me, but we were primarily involved in group functions within the singles ministry. The interest grew and we went out together. This worked for a season, but at one point I began to shut down emotionally and closed off. I struggled greatly with what was going on and felt so guilty that I was causing another painful situation to occur.

I certainly had my struggles and had met another man in our singles ministry that was gay and asking me questions. I didn't have any answers for him or for me. I heard a radio program in August of 1986 with a lady who had a son that was gay. It was on Focus on the Family so I wrote a letter asking for their information sheet on homosexuality. They sent a list of ministries, one of which was Love In Action. I wrote them a short letter asking for more information from them. Their response was a phone call asking if I might want to pursue a staff position as a House Leader.

I was ecstatic and believed that God had just showed me the next step in my life. So I pursued a staff position with Love In Action. I thought maybe this would be a place to explore what was going on in my heart and I would find others who would understand.

Moving to California to work with Love In Action was a VERY costly endeavor. I had two daughters I was leaving behind that were just 8 and 10 years old. I owned a home that I had to sell. I had over $30,000 from a severance settlement from my job. In my desire to find answers to lifelong questions, I chose to live on the savings and give everything else up and move 1500 miles away. I felt convicted that this was the right thing to do. It seemed the Lord was in it all, since there were unexplainable things that took place in order for all of this to happen. So I left my children, my family, and Nebraska and began a new life.

As I entered into my new home and community, I found a place we could talk more about things that were going on. This was very freeing for me because people had such similar experiences and we talked a lot about them. There was a heavy emphasis of healing and change regarding homosexuality. Since we were all hurting so much, that was good news! We learned that God loved us so much that He wanted to help us, to change us. So the emphasis was placed on a hope that God would heal us more, and tomorrow would be better.

When I left Nebraska, the relationship with the girl I was dating remained stuck and I felt by relocating the pressure would be relieved. And it was.

But after arriving in California, our communication continued through letters and telephone calls. Since the pressure was less, I opened up more, and we remained connected with regular contact. It felt good to have someone who cared about me. It helped me not to feel so alone in my new environment. It also provided something for the folks in the ministry to see that gave them hope for their own heterosexual possibilities. So we remained an item, and I talked about our relationship with those around me. There was a lot of encouragement to continue pursuing her.

I quickly became very involved in all of the things available through the ex-gay network. Conference after conference, teaching, healing prayer, healing seminars, seeking God deeply, fasting, hope upon hope that homosexuality would go away. If it didn't, we were taught to praise God anyway and continue on the journey.

I began to change for sure. But not as I had hoped. I learned how unhealthy my codependency was, and how it had harmed my former relationships. I learned that my behavior choices had caused many problems. I discovered that I had to find autonomy from my wounded family history. I discovered gifts and talents that had been hidden and began to see good things in who I am as a person.

The discovery of healthier communication, forgiveness, and release from things that held me back brought a lot of healing to my life. Daily reading of the Scriptures and other books, teaching, and prayer brought me to understand God's desire to be close to me were all extremely helpful. I grew in leaps and bounds into more of who I was created to be, which was very affirming.

But my internal struggles with being gay remained untapped and lingered underneath the surface. It was a looming secret waiting to come out at any moment. We learned to keep this awful beast at bay through staying away from temptations that were connected to it. It seemed I had to grasp that my homosexuality was an enemy of my soul and to fear its power to destroy my life. It was clear that the message was "Don't have any relationships with people who are 'unrepentant' homosexuals. Don't go near gay places or places where gay people hang out." We believed these things would draw you out and slide back into our old ways. As I looked across the bay at San Francisco, it had a dark and luminous sinful haze surrounding it in my mind. I believed it was the virtual center of everything that was the enemy of my soul.

Shortly after arriving in California I met a man who struck me deeply. I had felt very lonely and had prayed fervently for a friend. It seemed that he was an answer to my prayers. I began to pursue a relationship with him. He was a part of our ministry, so I felt it was OK to get to know him. The emotional fulfillment that I discovered became a major focus of my every waking hour. I looked forward to talks on the phone. We planned Saturday events together, and every hug that I could snag was a plus. Praying with him while holding hands was something that seemed to fit within the allowable standards, so I enjoyed that as well.

I called it a good friendship. I searched my heart for areas that might have been inappropriate while both of us continued to hang out together. It opened up a door to my heart that was very hard to close. I was confronted about the relationship being out of balance. But I believed that through working the bugs out, it could remain a healthy friendship.

As the relationship continued, I fantasized about what it could become if it were to go further. But of course this was far too close to the feared monster of homosexuality, so I disciplined my mind to stay away from those thoughts. As a result of the tension within me, conflicts came between us. I felt guilty, jealous, and ashamed because it was beginning to feel dangerous. Our leaders called it an emotionally dependent relationship and I began the process of repenting of the idolatry of the extreme nature of the relationship. All of this wounded both of us deeply. I called him to talk about the ways we were both being hurt and felt it best to not see him anymore. I had to push this away because of the pain it was bringing into my life.

I didn't want to go back into my old ways! Life back then was painful, and I assumed it was because I was gay. I didn't separate the unhealthiness part from the being gay part, and just lumped them all together. So I tried very hard to toe the line by isolating myself from anything that might have a slight growl or even hint of my painful past.

But the secret continued as a hole in my soul. I didn't feel there was any room to talk about this, so I continued to bury it and go to sleep at night with all of the confusion on my heart while asking God to remove it from my life.

I had developed some awesome relationships with people around me. Some of them are still friends today. I developed a good spiritual habit of Bible reading and prayer. I broadened my understanding of theology, church life, and a healthier sense of my part in the overall body of Christ. I learned about my family system and how it affected my development as a person.

I discovered I had a gift for writing, developing teaching outlines, and that I enjoyed public speaking. Computers had just become normal additions to the office environment, so I found my aptitude to be self-taught in software technology came in really handy! I learned about bookkeeping, office management, and payroll records. I have often said that my experience with Love In Action and Exodus became a practical replacement for a college degree.

I do not regret being a part of Love In Action and Exodus because there were many good things that came out of my roles there. Nonetheless, I am still sorting out the wounds that remain as a result of some of the perspectives that were taught. And I am still trying to work out my own homosexuality, since I really didn't get many answers about that within the ex-gay ministry. The answer I taught and believed was to push it away!

I remember hearing when I was a child that redheaded Irish girls are feisty. It seemed that included the premise that redheaded girls had bad tempers. As I grew to an adult I began to wonder which came first, the bad temper, or the red hair?

I've struggled my entire life with feeling different, being oversensitive about life and relationships, and not relating well to the world around me. I wanted desperately to be something different, to find a way to sort all of this out, but I didn't find any answers.

I finally realized I was gay. Shortly after I came out, I was taught that homosexuality is sin. So in conclusion I thought it might be possible to rid myself of this horrible thing called being gay. But there was an UGLY side affect to this way of thinking.

As I pursued the changes I hoped for, I reached a dead-end road. I found I couldn't shake something that went very deep inside me. I thought since I was gay, that I was bad! If homosexuality is sin, then I can only come to the deep, internal conclusion, that I am sin.

The deep level of shame, and lack of acceptance of myself as a person who is loved by God, kept me away from Him, and from myself. The oversensitivity didn't go away, the struggles of feeling inadequate and insignificant never seemed to lessen, and I continued to feel ashamed of my weakened state as a person.

This created a personal environment where I tried every way I could to cover the shame. I tried hard to wash it away, deny it, and stuff it.

My initial introduction to the You Can Change message sounded so good! "A new creature in Christ! . . . "And such were some of you!" Who wouldn't want that? It was all so very hopeful! Desirable! After all, if the red hair could go away with the freckles, then maybe the teasing would stop and I could now be like the others. Without a doubt, there are many red haired children who might have taken the option to change their freckles if it were possible.

But as the pursuit of change went on, same sex attractions didn't go away. There was no change in the understanding of same- or opposite-gender relationships. The unique understanding of feelings and relationships remained, and actually became more complex along with my increased state of shame from the perception that I was bad and unacceptable.

So now the message of change felt like a mandate: You must change! If homosexuality is a sin, and God hates sin, then the only way for God to love a homosexual would be to eradicate sin from one's life. So change meant to push it away somehow.

How can someone change something that is so deeply intertwined within themselves? Is it about sex? Is it about gender? Or is it more than all of that? I discovered I could change what I do sexually, so I did. I stopped having sex with men. I learned how to get along better with other men, and this helped me somewhat socially. However, I never related at a deep level. But the message of change seemed to beg more from me, a deeper change than I had come to experience after over 20 years of trying.

Underneath it all was a boiling anger, maybe even a type of rage inside my soul. "What in the hell do you want me to do? . . . I've been good. I've gone to all of the meetings, the conferences, counseling, intensive prayer. What else is there that You want from me?"

God wasn't changing me. So I remained sin, less valuable, less courageous. I remained damaged goods that were left with no options other than to learn how to suck it up and try my best to fit in, to assimilate into a world that seemed to understand itself. But I couldn't seem to understand myself.

Recently God has begun to shed light onto my heart. It seems that the point in all of this is that I am not sin. Well, that's good news! I am not intrinsically bad because I am gay. Well, that's good news too. It also seems that many of the things I used to say caused homosexuality were actually the result of being gay in a world that just didn't seem to connect.

One night I had a series of dreams that included vignettes of people showing their gifts, talents, and personality traits that were laying strangely separate from themselves. Some of these people were shedding some things, and pushing other things away. God began to enlighten me to things that He allowed, or created within my soul. Things that were unique, special, not ordinary. It seemed He was challenging me to stop trying to change myself and begin to learn to accept life as it is and see the value in it.

At a recent play called *The Boys Next Door*, my eyes welled up in tears when one of the boys stood up, shedding the effects of being a special needs kid, and talked about what it was like to live in his world. He began to talk about the things he brought to life in those around him and how he was being used in his very own special way to enhance life.

I immediately resonated with his heart. I realized that there was a silver lining in the rain cloud of being gay. I am uniquely created by God. He has somehow allowed me to be gay, and He promises He will bring good out of all situations for His glory—and He says it will be good for me too! He has a special place for me, and my being gay fits into the bigger picture of who I am. To remove it would be to remove a part of myself as God created me to be.

The ugly is that so many within the Christian culture and community have touted the message that gays must change, that being gay is sin, and gays are truly going to lose out on God's kingdom unless they change. The double bind is a burden far too weighty for anyone to carry.

The message of change sets the tone for people to try very hard to comply with its demands. Yet they find on the other side of their attempts failure of great magnitude—a message that they will never measure up to God's standards for acceptance.

I received an email from a pastor who has been at odds with my writings. He wrote: "John, maybe the problem is that these gay folks just haven't prayed long enough to fight against this and win the victory."

Steam came out of my ears when I read that! I felt incensed! Obviously, this man has never really heard the heart and soul of gay people. I don't think I know of anyone who prays as hard, stands as strongly, and endures as long as many within the gay community.

If you ask any gay person who has gone to a Christian for help, the thing that they hear the loudest is: "Pray, and read your Bible more." There isn't anything more demeaning than to say that to a struggling gay person. Many of them know the Bible very well and can quote chapter and verse, and show you the calluses on their knees from praying.

I'm not denying there is hope for change! Please hear me. In our life journey, we do experience changes in our personalities, our desires, and some of the seemingly intrinsic features we have carried along with us. And yes, some people do experience changes in their sexuality. I will not deny the uniqueness of each person's life in Christ and the things that God may do.

The challenge to look at is this: What is the motivation for the message of change? Is it to see someone experience the goodness in God? Or is it to somehow eradicate being gay from our life, or someone else's?

Is the motivation to rid someone of the burden of being gay so that the shame will go away? Do we want desperately to remove a gay orientation from someone's life because it seems to be difficult for them? Do we want to change people who are gay because we are uncomfortable being around them?

Think about this: Is it better to help people accept life as it is—gay or not? Is it better to look at someone in their heart and say, "God loves you right where you are. He has a life for you that is amazing. If you will pursue Him, He will show you the way. Quit worrying about change, and join His pathway of life for you. Seek Him with all of your heart, and He will guide you."

The real lie that has created the greatest problem is the frontline message that gays can change. I am coming to believe that the true attack from the enemy of our souls stems from the message of change that many understand as, you must change. If the enemy can get people to believe that unless they change they will never be acceptable to God, then he has found the way to consign them to a lifetime of shame and degradation.

You see, it is this kind of internal shame that brings overcompensating behaviors that are destructive, dehumanizing, and just overall unhealthy. The enemy of our soul loves to see gay people, who are so talented, sensitive, and insightful, feel trapped in a never- ending bind of self-destruction. So in setting up the message of change that most likely will never be fulfilled, he has the lock and the key is thrown away.

Let me repeat this. When gay people think because they are gay they are intrinsically flawed, the shame builds. To cover the shame we subsequently see in people's lives addictive practices, inflated and extreme lifestyles. So many times the answer from the Christian community is change, and it will all get better.

Out of sincere desire and motivation the journey to seek first the kingdom of change ensues. This path comes to no end and therefore the shame only goes deeper.

In an energetic search for change I found a cover of being the good boy, the great Christian leader, the moral one. I gave myself no permission to show ugly emotions or to make undesirable mistakes. I stayed away from anything that might in any way reflect negatively upon my reputation.

Internally, I already felt so ashamed and broken I couldn't afford anything that might add to that already heavy load.

As I am allowing myself to be more authentic, the pretty exterior is falling off. My reputation is being called into question, and I am no longer fearful of making a mistake. As I accept that I am gay and am willing to let that out, I find that many pressures are falling off.

What is the answer?

The answer is to find God's love in who we are, in how we've been created (or allowed to be created) and to rid ourselves of the misappropriated shame from being gay. I have recently come to know many people who now accept themselves, with God's tremendous love, as being gay. In this transition from shamed, to loved, many of the destructive behaviors miraculously cease. Drugs are thrown away, sexually addictive behaviors stop, relationships get better, and people begin to thrive in their relationship with God.

There is a battle, but who has been deceived? Of course, the enemy doesn't want anyone to find freedom from destruction. So the battle rages on between the culture who says, change is necessary and the culture who says, you are loved as you are. There is certainly a war going on for the souls of those who are gay.

I want to see more freedom from the destruction. Do you?

A very helpful book for me has been *The Velvet Rage: Overcoming the Pain of Growing Up Gay in a Straight Man's World,* by Alan Downs, Ph.D.

The Love In Action Staff and Clients - Part 6

I acknowledge YOU! I acknowledge that the many changes I have gone through in these years since I left Love In Action have caused challenging reactions for some of you. I have retracted some things I taught with passion when I led groups or teachings within Love In Action. I realize this may have caused you to doubt or to experience confusion. I also realize it may bring up some challenging thoughts about where I am today.

When I was a brand-new Christian, and beginning to follow Christ, He brought me to the deathbed of a man who had AIDS. After he passed away, I sat, wept, and pleaded with God to give me a way to walk alongside the gay community. I wanted desperately to help bring hope, to bring restoration with Jesus.

This intimate time with Jesus has called me forward for 25 years and continues to do so today. Nothing has changed there!

My greatest prayer for Love In Action participants has always been that each of you would find a life worthy of the calling of Jesus Christ. This is still my prayer. Regardless of what I believe, or teach, it is my hope that you will faithfully follow Jesus!

I've spent a significant amount of time reading through a thorough list of people who have gone through the residential program at Love In Action. At my best count, there are 461! It has been my privilege to have known each one.

We prayed together, cried together, shared significant times of intimate discussion, and have an eternal relationship based on a shared life experience.

I am in current contact with around 130 of these folks. Through Face-Book, emails, and personal interaction, I am extremely grateful to have these connections Sadly, 16 have passed away. But, 41 are married to the opposite gender, 80 publicly identify as being gay of which 12 have acknowledged having a committed, same-sex partnership.

There are many I haven't connected with; however, what I do know is interesting for sure. These men and women are significant people in my life and I care about them to the point where I have an interest in continuing to know them, pray for them, and hopefully be with them in eternity.

Going all the way back to 1986, I can actually say I had some of my best times in life with people who were around Love In Action during those years.

There are seasons in my experience with Love In Action. Love In Action was in California from 1986 through 1994. Then the Memphis years began and continued through 2008. The experiences with each season were dramatically different from each other. The California years were very relationship oriented. We all hung out together, spent lots of time around food, fun, laughter, and knowing one another intimately. We also had some very serious times with Jesus, and some challenging times where we worked through the stuff that would come up within our relationships.

On the other hand, the Memphis years became more clinical, therapeutic, and a sense of community surrounded the clients but the staff and I remained distant. There were great times within the houses, but the staff kept further away so as to somehow be more healthy with regards to professionalism and counseling. Many of my personal memories of program members are stronger from the California years, but I have some great life experiences from Memphis as well.

I see your faces regularly as I go through photo albums that I have kept. I think about you as I recount your stories and many of the discussions I remember having with you. I picture places like The Lord's Land, San Francisco, Sacramento, the redwood forests, beaches, hikes, and so many others from the California years. Most of the pictures in my mind in Memphis are of a more formal nature—deep revelations, family growth, and spiritual changes encountered together.

Today, from my life at Love In Action, I have friends in countries far and wide! Finland, Africa, Brazil, Canada, Japan, New Zealand, Australia, India, The Netherlands, England, Germany, El Salvador, Spain, and even Azerbaijan.

Nonetheless, your names, lives, and hearts are indelibly inked to my soul. Do I remember you? Of course I do! I have hundreds of pictures from the California years but when the Memphis program changed and developed I made an effort to find some other ways to remember you. For the Memphis clients, I endeavored to remember you through our graduation coins kept in the Ark of the Covenant in the office. This was my way of keeping you close and not to be forgotten. How many times did we support others who Crossed over Jordan?

Honestly, I grieved often that the professional boundaries kept me away from knowing the Memphis people more deeply. I never liked having to remain therapeutically separated. I always struggled with having counselors who handled their client load while I became more of an administrator of the ministry. What I always loved about being part of the ministry of Love In Action was the depth of relationship that was so significant. In the later years that seemed to get lost, and I became more and more dissatisfied with my role in the ministry as it transitioned away from the former years.

Through the pressure of becoming more professional, we lost the intimacy that many of us had known so deeply in California. Actually, I think many others also struggled with that transition to a professionally oriented program.

From all those years ago, it was always my greatest heart's desire to provide a place for healing, a place for spiritual growth, and to encourage a stronger faith in God. I believed I could relate to those who came to us. I related to their struggle with homosexuality. I had experienced actions that were unhealthy and relationship challenges and the struggle with despair that were so common for us to share about.

It was from this motivation that I went to Love In Action every day. I believed I was creating an environment for men and women to find a healthier life which always included a drastic separation from anything related to homosexuality.

I believe many amazing and wonderful things happened in the groups, counseling offices, and the intimate times spent in the residential environment. I also believe there were times of feeling heard and validated for many of the program participants. I know for certain that many of them found a deeper and more valid relationship with God as a result of being involved with Love In Action.

Every time I came up with a new concept, I taught it with the hope that we would become more effective at reaching the intended goal of a closer walk with the Lord, or a greater peace with life and relationships. As I have written all of these articles on acknowledging things I regret, or that I've done wrong, I think back over why I did what I did in the first place.

I am only now getting in touch with a deep reality of the true pain and discouragement that can come along with being gay. As I reach down into my own heart and soul, I find the deeper life experience that from my position as the Director of Love In Action I couldn't seem to find. I remained in my head so much of the time, trying to be strong, stable, and effective.

Over these last three years I have discovered so many things about myself that I wish I had known many years ago. I feel discouraged that these things were so hidden from my own heart because it wasn't possible to have given them out.

There were some marriages that formed which today are blessed, intimate, and fulfilling families. Beautiful children have been born and loved by people who grew healthier from their time at Love In Action. Marriages that had been devastated by broken lives were wonderfully restored. Some of my fond memories included relationships between parents and their kids that were restored, discovering new and more genuine connections with each other. It was during these times when I experienced the tearful reality of God's amazing grace to renew, heal, and restore lives and relationships.

Some of those who were single found new careers, brand-new foundations through which they discovered meaning and purpose. Some others became ministry leaders, others found restoration to former ministry passions.

There were a few people who discovered public ministry service and gained great notoriety within the Christian culture. Then some worked behind the scenes as amazing encouragers and reconcilers within God's kingdom.

There were some incredible changes that occurred in people's lives that were involved in our support group ministries. Hundreds of people came to our support groups in the Bay Area of Northern California. I can see them walking through the doors each week as though it were yesterday.

There was a group of about 20 men who were involved in an intensive support group that met in San Rafael, California. The majority of these men have remained in contact with each other through the years. Fortunately, I am also in contact with many of them. It is wonderful to consider many of them friends today. To be honest, most of those men have now found their faith to be reconciled with being gay and continue to support one another along that path. Several of them are living on long-term, faith- centered, partnered relationships.

In Memphis, we had a large group of people who were part of our Radical Living program, where God did some awesome and amazing things in their lives. These included some who didn't struggle with homosexuality, parents, and ministry leaders who took the challenges that were placed in front of them and grew tremendously. I hear from them as well, about how much their lives changed for the better as a result of being part of Radical Living.

At one point we had a local support group of 25 to 30 people involved that provided a place for discovery and growth. We also held support ministries for parents and loved ones that provided a safe place to find camaraderie and support with others who understood. I know that this produced healing and connections that increased the tent pegs of God's Kingdom.

I fully acknowledge that within my time at Love In Action, God did amazing things. In all of my energy in acknowledging things that I believe I've done wrong, it has never been my intent to wash all of these years away as though there was no purpose nor value gained. Much good has come from all of those years.

I want to appeal to all of those who celebrate their time with Love In Action. I want you to consider something that is very important. For those who didn't come away with the results that you did, many are really hurting, lonely, and have desperate pain that has yet to be healed. There are others who have found solace in accepting that they are gay and have gone on with God feeling that part of their life issues have been resolved.

We are a diverse people from many paths that life has brought our way. We are brothers and sisters along life's road. No matter what seems to be in front of us, it is very important to remember that God's grace is abundant and His love never fails.

I also want to again reiterate to those who were clients of Love In Action, if you'd like to contact me with questions or comments or just to chat, please do so. I've enjoyed reconnection with numerous people in these last couple of years and it has helped me and hopefully them as well. I am on FaceBook, and my website has numerous ways to connect with me—phone, email, and a contact form.

> "I urge you to live a life worthy of the calling you have received. Be completely humble and gentle; be patient, bearing with one another in love. Make every effort to keep the unity of the Spirit through the bond of peace" (Ephesians 4:1-3, NIV).

Over the many years of my involvement with Love In Action, I had the privilege to work with some incredible and dedicated staff. Men and women who spent their hearts and lives to walk alongside some very special people living in some deeply challenging life circumstances. I've never questioned their dedication, or their motives for their sacrificial service through Love In Action. House Managers who lived and breathed the daily lives of our clients and made a huge significant impact for their good.

There were counselors, or staff workers as we eventually called them, who gave their heart and soul to the individual counseling and growth processes of each client they took under their wing.

Our staff were dedicated to their relationship with God and desired so much to see each person grow to know Him personally and receive His love. With intensity each one energetically gave to the clients every-thing they had to give.

Sadly, the premise of the ministry was so focused on eradicating homo-sexuality from the life of the client that the outcomes were stifled and they became discouraged very often. Due to the intensity of the per-sonal relationships with each client, the sense of failure and exhaustion became very stressful and we had a lot of staff turnover.

I want to acknowledge the wonderful people who served Love In Action throughout my time with the ministry and their gift of time and talent to the ministry.

My Daughters - Part 7

When my first apology appeared on FaceBook, my older daughter wrote a very poignant comment. She said, "Dad, it's too bad you spent so much time trying to fix something that didn't need to be fixed. Think about all that you lost out on."

I was shocked to read her words, and challenged to the core of my being. I knew exactly what she was saying and I didn't read it with me in mind, but for what she was saying about her own life. I think she was actually telling me how she felt about losing her dad for all of those years.

When I left Omaha in 1986 to move to California to work with Love In Action I was deeply torn. But instead of showing my true sense of loss, I just covered it up and kept the blue sky approach out in front. I remember when I told my daughters I would be moving out of town I just talked about all of the things I could think of that might be positive. Honestly, there weren't many to speak of. I knew that these two little girls of just eight and ten years old would miss their daddy terribly. I knew I would miss them terribly. But all of the surrounding circumstances seemed to point that God was in charge and leading me to make this move. Frankly I didn't know what else to do.

My older daughter was always the more out spoken one. She often embodied the serious things about life and brought them out with conviction. My younger daughter seemed to float above the fray of life. So as I listen to them, the older one seemed to bring the temperature gauge to my heart. I have continued to remain curious as to what my younger daughter actually felt through the years because it has been most often the older one that has brought it out.

As I look at my departure from Omaha, it was a decision I am not sure I would have made today. If I did, I might have tried to make it a shorter term than over twenty years! What my daughter was referring to was so much greater than I had ever allowed myself to think about. It was too huge for me to process.

Frequently when I was in California I would ask for prayer and tried desperately to understand God's purpose in me being so far away from my daughters. Others would tell me that God was taking care of them and that I needn't worry about their lives. This made sense on one level, but underneath I knew that they were missing out and so was I. Each birthday, special event or Christmas, I knew that I was 1500 miles away from them. As the years passed I felt the chasm growing broader and broader between us.

Oh, yes, I was missing out on something, but after just a few years and as they grew older I felt the pain, the distance, and the self protection grow as I looked into their faces. I was gone from their lives, but I hadn't died, so there was no way to grieve the real pain each time I showed up in their lives.

At one point a special birthday was coming and I tried really hard to put together a birthday-in-a-box with the hope it would be received as intended and would say, I Love You. But I never heard anything about it and I felt completely defeated. I just didn't know what to do. I tried other things through the years, but never realized that it wasn't the gifts, or the special attention, it was the separation between us that was at the root of all of the pain.

I continued to try to rationalize my distance. At one point I figured God wanted to get rid of the homosexuality in my life so that I could be a better dad for them. I believed that certainly I would not be a good dad as a gay man, so I was in the long term program to somehow find that better dad for my daughters.

When my older daughter was in her late teens I wrote a news letter about how wonderful our family workshops at Love In Action had been. But then, once again, the temperature gauge came out: "Dad, here you are trying to help other families be healthier when you can't even work on your own." The pain spoken through a little girls heart pounded against my chest. She was right! I was doing a very poor job on my own family because I was so distant, and the miles between us seemingly prevented any kind of reconciliation between us.

I was trying to fix something that didn't need to be fixed! My homosexuality never went away but I continued to try to figure this out. Why? Why did it seem so right to go away and get help? What was God up to? Why was there a seeming confirmation for my work with Love In Action when my own daughters were in so much pain?

In my own heart, I tried to work it out. I saw these little girls grow into teenagers. I spent so little time with them that I could not in any way know their hearts. The trust had been severely broken and yet I prayed, and prayed for some wisdom as to how to show them I loved them.

When my older daughter became a mature teen I did what I thought a good Christian dad would do. I bought her a beautiful ring to give to her as a symbol of her own chastity as she entered into the dating world. I believed it would make a difference to her life. I thought she would cherish that ring because it came from me.

But now, with her words ringing in my ears, I see that it was likely a farce to her. How would this ring and a message about her purity mean anything to her without relationship behind it? How would I know what was significant about her sexuality when I never met any of the boys she dated in high school?

And yet, I continued to believe that underneath there somewhere, my daughters loved me. I hoped that they saw something positive about me and that someday there would be a connection, and reconciliation of hearts where we could know one another again. If in fact God was making me a better man, they would see that in time, and maybe they could move beyond their grief and loss to see the finished product of God's intervention in my sexuality. I mean, I wouldn't be gay any longer and they would respect this new man of faith and morality.

That is until I read her words, and felt her heart. She wasn't interested in me changing my sexuality and becoming straight. She needed her daddy throughout the years and I was gone. I blamed many other things through the years for what had happened to separate us but the reality was, I just wasn't there.

I had deemed that what I had believed was the sin of homosexuality had to be eradicated from my life. Since this was of primary importance, other things like my daughters had to take second place to that.

Of course, today, after the damage is done, I grieve that I didn't know more about God, about His grace, and about His love back then. I feel devastated about what has been lost in my relationship with two beautiful little girls that are now mothers to my incredible four grand children.

As I evaluated my own childhood experiences something hit me between the eyes. When I was two and a half, my parents separated and it wounded me greatly. When my younger daughter was two and a half, I divorced her mother and her life was devastated. When my oldest grandson was just two and a half, my daughter and her husband were divorced and it changed his life forever.

Oh, my, how the generations are impacted over and over again by the abandonment of relationship. I feel deeply grieved to see how confusion, and separation have wounded my own life, and three generations of distance have come about.

Have I really tried to fix something that didn't need to be fixed in the first place and subsequently lost a whole generation of love and care? My dad was an amazing man and my daughters loved him dearly. He passed away in 1997 and they still miss his love for them and feel the loss. I wanted so deeply to be the kind of man he was and have my daughters love me like they loved him. This was a large part of the motivation to get my life fixed! I kept dreaming that some day they would appreciate my hard work and attempt to be a better man.

The pain is still present, though lessened I hope. There is a glimmer of change in our relationships. As we've grown older the edge has been rounded off some. But I can see now just once more how the consequences of the rigidity of right wing Christianity has wounded me and my family.

As my outspoken daughter also told me, "Dad, remember when we used to go to church every Sunday and sit on the front row? We hated that. We also hated the loud preacher we had to listen to every Sunday as his spit came out into the crowd."

Well, once again, I heard something I didn't know about her experience with church. No wonder she doesn't go to church today? Why would she? She was wrangled into church for several years with me paying no attention to what my little kids might have been thinking. I thought they enjoyed it! I was blind and not listening to them.

I responded to her honest comments with, "You know what? I didn't like him either. I hated his yelling and I often felt like I was being scolded for my sin." I also explained the front row as being necessary since we were interpreting for our hearing impaired friend. I hope that that conversation made some difference. I wanted to at least acknowledge her thoughts and show her that I could relate to them.

An unfinished work continues as I hope I work all of this through for myself. As I do, I also hope my daughters will come and join me a little bit more each day. I love them dearly and grieve the loss almost every day of my life. It is one of the most painful realities of my past. As God continues to reveal to me His grace, I hope I can give that to them. Maybe there will be a day when we are closer. I hope so.

Mixed Orientation Marriage

December 2011

It's our 23rd wedding anniversary this month. As I continue to process this adjustment of life and reality, I began to look back over my relationship with my second wife, Vileen. When we first met, we enjoyed each other, the discussions and the lightheartedness of life. As soon as we began dating it all changed. Soon, my heart closed off and I felt terrible. I couldn't figure out what had happened to shut me down. I tried as hard as I could to search my heart for answers but to no avail, I just couldn't figure this out and I was in a lot of fear about it.

A few months later I discovered ex-gay ministries and amazingly was invited to apply for a position on staff with Love In Action. I felt relieved of the stress and off I went to my new horizon! Whatever had caused my heart to shut down seemed to go away and we were back to easy conversation, sharing letters upon letters and it seemed it was all good. Visits in California and trips back home to Omaha seemed to bring us back to normal but the long distance relationship was stressful. I was given the advice to make a decision about the relationship. It seemed that I was waffling on any movement forward and due to the long distance between us, it was clear that without a further commitment, such as a marriage proposal, it might be unwise to continue.

I wasn't ready for marriage so I decided something had to change. The title of dating changed to friendship and we continued to talk periodically . It was odd that it didn't feel any different but I didn't question that. Then, it seemed that my heart was desiring something more. After a special interchange between us at Christmas time, my heart opened up again and I truly thought that Vileen was the one I was to marry.

After a very romantic proposal of marriage at sunset on the Pacific Ocean, my heart remained open through the next several months and all seemed a go. But then came the last minute events including a couple's wedding shower. During the shower the glasses clinked and the crowd insisted on a kiss between the two of us. We had never kissed and it seemed so awkward and contrived. The applause and unrelenting pressure brought me to no options. The first kiss wasn't enough for the audience, so there were two kisses required that day.

I felt mortified! I felt so embarrassed and it was not comfortable, nor was it a good memory. But rather, an uncomfortable beginning to the deeper physical challenges of our relationship that would come later.

We entered into lots of talks and pre-marital counseling with our local pastor took place, but the physical side of the relationship wasn't addressed. Finances, living arrangements and such were all discussed, but still no talk of what would soon become the sexual aspects of our marriage. The counsel I received on sexuality from ex-gay mentors was, "Oh, don't worry, the plumbing will work, when the time is right."

The honeymoon was in a beautiful place, who wouldn't love Hawaii in a brand new luxurious hotel? Right? Wrong. Sex was uncomfortable, strange, and once again not natural or comfortable. It was just chalked up to a new relationship, an adjustment to someone else's sexuality that hadn't been explored before. I thought it was just natural to experience this discomfort and strangeness. Others had told me their honeymoon was difficult so I tried really hard not to crumble under the discouragement.

Soon, the struggle deepened, and a tremendous fear set in. Fear of failure, fear of performance expectations, fear of making a terrible mistake. I was beginning to curse the homosexuality that seemed to pervade my life with darkness, pain and misery. I cried out, "God, why does this stupid homosexuality have to always cause problems. Can't you take it away?"

The pressure to perform continued and the emotional and personal angst was more than I could bear. In prayer after prayer I pleaded with God to help, to do something. But this was something I didn't talk about, not with anyone.

The pressure lessened over time and sex became less of an issue, but there was also no passion, spontaneity or lust for my wife. Our intimate life was perfunctory and yet it seemed, as I was told, the plumbing worked. But the embarrassment didn't lessen. Sex, nakedness, bodies, romance all seemed to be severely lacking a natural function, or desire. It all seemed so strange to me. Try as I might, I never felt sexually attracted to my wife and this included romantic attraction outside of the bedroom.

When I was involved in gay relationships there was no shame, no embarrassment or discomfort. It felt so natural and I desired to be close, naked, and sexual with another man. As a good Christian man, I chocked that up to forbidden knowledge and believed God could certainly not bless something like that. But as I compared my homosexual past with my marriage one sure seemed more natural and desirable than the other.

I had to just keep pushing it away, forbidding myself to think about it, or to desire it. Living the sacrificial life of a Christ follower included denying my same sex desires or even having thoughts of being emotionally close to another man. I had to keep it safe and stay away from other men who were like me, unless there was a professional connection.

Then another change in our lives occurred after about 10 years that caused things to shift. Due to further embarrassment about our sexual relationship, it all slowed to a minimal occurrence. This lessened the extreme pressure, but increased the fears, anxiety and shame.

Now that our sexual life was virtually non-existent there was another level of shame that came about. I had been known as one who was delivered from homosexuality and now was successful in marriage. This had to include a successful sex life too! But there wasn't one. So I went into hiding about that. Anytime there was discussion of marriage within friendships, or men's gatherings I felt the blood rise to my head, I felt fearful of being found out. What if they asked me about how often we had sex? And when other men talked about their own glorious romance and sexual frequency, I was jealous, anxious, and more shame was attached to my woefully inadequate life as a married man. I wasn't measuring up to what people thought about me. Was my testimony a scam? It'll get better - won't it?

Yes, I had deep levels of shame. I never felt normal, nor did I connect with other men on their sexuality, marriages, or life in general. I believed that if I related enough, pressed through enough, found enough courage, it would get better! I believed our marriage would grow, change and mature to a place of normalcy. I was told, many years ago, that there was a 20 year warm up with sex and marriage and that at some point it would all come together.

It didn't get better. It became harder, more uncomfortable, more of a daily challenge . I truly didn't believe my life was like anyone else's. My marriage was abnormal, dysfunctional and yet there was a ying, yang that seemed to work okay at a practical level. But each night as I got into bed, I experienced the all too familiar pressure to perform and to have a healthy physical marriage, and ours wasn't.

Year after year, the emotional closeness was challenging, my desire was not growing and our relationship was a struggle and not what most believe to be marriage bliss.

Two attempts to talk about it seemed to fail to bring any resolution or change. With great fear and trepidation the subject was approached. With a burst of great vulnerability I attempted to discuss the absence of sexuality, physical desire, and the fears and anxiety that seemed to permeate our relationship. But in the end, it didn't seem to come across or get at the root of what was really happening to cause this awful turmoil that plagued me every day of my life. I see now, it was because I didn't understand the root causes of our struggles, and therefore kept it hidden underneath and unexposed even to myself.

WOW, the answer!

Shame! Shame of growing up gay in a straight man's world! That's it!! All those years ago, I lived in the shame of being gay in a world that didn't understand me, didn't know how to relate to me, or encourage me.

The ex-gay world didn't have the answers either! If you couldn't talk about what was really going on underneath, how would you figure it out? It would be impossible with those constraints in place. The plumbing will work. What's up with that? Is that all it is, plumbing? Certainly not! It is relationship of the very most vulnerable kind. It can be threatening, fearful, and full of anxiety because of the lack of compatibility with the opposite gender.

Yes, shame. Shame of not being like the others. Shame of being something that was strange to many and misunderstood by most. Shame that I was created weird, broken, dysfunctional. Something deep, and insurmountable is intrinsically wrong with me. Can this ever be fixed? Can the homosexuality go away?

I believed that with enough prayer, counsel, obedience, and risk, that this, the marriage, would get better. I hoped that my sexuality would change, it would mature, and grow. I hoped that someday I would eventually find my way through this dark tunnel of mixed up development and sexuality. But that someday, never came and it became increasingly worse, more threatening and more silent.

The stuffing of feelings, desires, hope, and natural living seemed to become a way of life. I was dying, shrinking away from myself, and from others. I had no answers other than to somehow get rid of what I was feeling. I was taught to deny myself and follow Christ, and I did the best I could to do that! This meant that there would be no room to explore, or search for the real me because the real me was deemed as shameful and broken.

Yes, it was shame that I felt at that first kiss. It was shame I felt each time I felt the pressure to perform sexually, or to be romantic, or to get close. It was shame I felt each night when I would disrobe in private so as to not expose myself to what I was really feeling. It was shame I felt each time I participated in a men's function, or couples discussion about marriage or family. It was shame I felt each Monday morning I attended session after session of the Men's Fraternity with the men who seemed to relate to its value in their lives.

I spent over twenty five years attempting to mask the shame, the fear, the dysfunction and broken heart. Through all of those years there were plenty of people to support my dysfunction. There were words of affirmation, commendation, and positional authority to affirm how well I was living in self control against my homosexuality. I was the hero, the one who made it! I had the story of an ex-gay icon.

But, shame again permeated my role as a leader, my achievements, and my performance in ministry. I hadn't arrived! My life was nothing like many thought it was, the embarrassment I felt each day regarding my body, sexuality, and subsequently my marriage was deeply hidden from public view! I wouldn't breathe a word to anyone for fear of further shame if they knew. Certainly no one could know my secret.

My cover-up system worked so well. That is until I was free from the system being the leader of Love In Action and therefore free to expose my undiscovered reality. My position was broken, the role in leadership went away and the support structures that existed to hold my denial in place were gone. Then it all broke loose! A little at a time, but delicately my Lord allowed me to see underneath the layers of my life.

I found the freedom to become more honest with myself. I began to discover my own inner truth. I was gay. That's it! I've always been gay. The shame didn't begin when I was an adult, it was always there. I have always felt the shame of being different in a world that didn't know what to do with me.

So, now what? What's next in my life. How do I now integrate the real me?

Honestly, I am figuring that out day by day. But the deconstruction has begun. In order for me to live sincerely.

I must move past the facades that have been in place. I can see today how many things in life are no longer a fit for me because they aren't me and never have been. They were my camouflaged screen. But I am not willing to hide any longer and I am choosing to find the back room of life rooted in shame.

I Fired the Shame Committee

January 2012

The world is not a gay friendly world. I know, no surprise here. But as I think about my life as a gay person, the disconnect has always caused me to struggle and believe there was something wrong with me from the inside out.

So, I decided to fire the Shame Committee. I can do nothing about being gay. I was gay, I am gay, and I will be gay for the duration of my lifetime. You might be reacting right now to the term gay assuming that this means something about my actions or my behavior, but it doesn't. Being gay for me is not just about having sex. It is about an intrinsic part of my being that goes back to my first awareness of life. It is a filter that has impacted virtually every aspect of my being. It has been there all along and my responses have led to many shameful reactions that I decided I no longer want to accept.

I desire to integrate the facets of my life into one being. I am sensitive to the thoughts and feeling of others. I am discerning about wrongdoing and when people are emotionally wounded. I am creative, love bright colors and beauty! I love artistic design. I don't like physically threatening activity and believe that God did not create any of us to harm one another.

I am intuitive about challenges, love to see things improve in the lives of people, and care deeply about those who are bound in discouragement and shame.

I find the heart, the soul, and the body of a man very attractive. I find it very difficult to relate to a man who has shut down his emotions and sees the world through a closed soul.

I need the affirmation of other gay men who understand what it is like to grow up gay. They can relate to my heart and life experience. I find that personal tension and angst seems to melt away when I am in the company of other gay men. I relax and can be more naturally myself in those settings. It is even better when they are men who can relate to having a strong faith and belief in God's love for us and who embrace His salvation.

I have decided that I am not going to accept that being gay is sinful. I will no longer believe that my life is less valuable than any others that are straight. My sexual orientation as a gay man is spiritually neutral. It came into my life unannounced and without request. It is part of my personal formation and it does not in and of itself mean I am living in sin.

There is absolutely NOTHING in the bible that says there is anything wrong with being born with a same sex orientation. Nothing is said about people with alternative sexual orientations with the exception of Jesus addressing the circumstances of the eunuchs which he does not judge or say anything negative about. He only says:

> Jesus replied, "Not everyone can accept this word (about heterosexual marriage), but only those to whom it has been given. For there are eunuchs who were born that way, and there are eunuchs who have been made eunuchs by others—and there are those who choose to live like eunuchs for the sake of the kingdom of heaven. The one who can accept this should accept it."
> Matthew 19:11-13

I consider myself aligned with the eunuchs of Jesus' day. Yes I am married, but my circumstances are different than a heterosexual's. I now see that Jesus didn't condemn the eunuchs, and I am no longer going to sit under condemnation because I am gay.

Much like the rest of what I've written in these journals, I am still asking God for His surprises along my journey. Where will He lead me next? I frankly don't know. 2008 was a year of the unknown and boy, was it full of surprises! So, after admitting that I am gay God will assuredly bring on more things that I didn't expect. I hope He is at work fulfilling my heart's desire.

What is my heart's desire? At this time, I want to discover what it is to live an integrated life, including being authentic about being gay, but many other things as well. What does it mean to be an authentic John Smid? My journey will reveal that to me along the way.

My life has been full of hiding and attempting to be what others want me to be. Today I just want to learn to embrace and enjoy who I am. It is my hope that I will continue to grow to be a well adjusted, gay man. After all of these years trying to get rid of my homosexuality, I hope that it won't take too long to find peace with it all.

In January 2012, I decided to attend my first Gay Christian Network conference in Orlando, Florida. I was asked to be a part of a panel discussion about ex-gay ministry. I was with a couple of other former Exodus leaders. This was the first time I actually used the word gay in public to describe myself. It just came out and so did I.

From that point on I made a distinct stand on the ground. I said it, and meant it. Saying I was gay had a whole lot more to do with how I felt inside, than it did what I did or didn't do sexually. When I made that statement something shifted inside me that was positive. I said it! I didn't die, and now everyone who heard me knows it.

Admitting that I am in a mixed orientation marriage was also more of a public way of relating to so many other men and women who are married to someone who is straight. I felt it significant to bring that out so that anyone else who hadn't thought about that before could hear those words. A year or so earlier when I first heard that term it seemed to comfort me. I felt connected to some other people's life experience and didn't feel so alone. I moved further into a sense of confidence afterwards.

Yes, I relate to the fire hydrant from Kevyn's photo collection. My life was laid in place to have significance in the ex-gay world for a season, but now the season is changed. The fire hydrant and all of its underpinnings are seemingly no longer needed. It is time to deconstruct their parts and see where they fit today.

Alan Downs talks about times in life where we have the option to continue to grow forward, or to foreclose and remain stuck. I have felt the anxiety of the temptation to foreclose on circumstances that are just too tough to go through, but I am making the choice not to foreclose.

In reviewing the last several years there is a lot of new information I've gained about how to respond to those who are gay. I've changed a lot in what it means to live a grace filled life for myself.

I recently got in touch with some very painful feelings about my faith from 30 years ago. When I first realized that God loved me, offered me eternal life, and began to learn about the life of Jesus I was so excited! I was an energetic evangelist and wanted so much for others to find the exciting news I had found.

I had accepted that I was gay, and in a childlike way, I received God's love and didn't feel ashamed. But a lot has happened in the last 30 years.

The Big Black Box of Shame

June 2012

After much review of what has been written within these pages, and what I've learned, I've recently begun doing some work with a counselor to help me sort all of this out. After a few sessions and a healing weekend to accelerate my progress, I've developed some awareness and would like to close with this summary.

It was 1982 and I was at the end of a deeply emotionally wounding relationship. I had nowhere to turn and someone suggested I attend an al-anon meeting for gay men. I heard it was a better place to go than to the local bars to find some solace and healing.

So I went. I found encouragement, safety, and others who could relate to me at the time. I also found personal prayer to a God who really did care about my life. Due to many connections during that season of my life, I was introduced to a living relationship with a God who saved me from my human circumstances. I also discovered new understanding in the Bible and enjoyed reading about the life of Jesus.

I was so excited about my new focus in life that I told everyone about what I had found! It was so freeing to me to learn that I no longer had to worry about where I would go when I died. I continued to engage in dating same sex relationships and often engaged in sex but in the end, I would also often tell them about Jesus!

I was gay. I was out. I was comfortable being gay. And, I now called myself a Christian! I felt released from so many things including healing from a lot of pain from the unhealthy relationships.

That is until I entered a church community. I was hungry to discover others like myself who understood my new faith. I was immature in my knowledge of the church and Christian beliefs. I just knew I needed to find others who could relate to me. I also knew that I needed a time away from places where I had been unhealthy and the association with other bar flies that I had grown accustomed to knowing. And, I needed a break from the unhealthy gay relationships.

I found a singles ministry within a church I was introduced to. It seemed to be a safe place for me to land. So, I began to listen to the teaching, and hear the messages from those in the community. Since I was coming from an identity of being gay, my ears often turned to anything that was said, or taught about my particular persuasion. The singles pastor and those I met were really awesome. They provided me a place where I could be honest with those closest to me. The teaching was helpful and practical and I didn't hear too much there about homosexuality.

However, within the church at large, the messages began to come in clear. I was given a Big Black Box of Shame. I quickly began to experience the message that I had to change. I had to somehow no longer be gay.

Since I had been in such pain, and was really ignorant, the lessons I began to hear and believe were that my pain was primarily from my being gay. I began to believe that if I could eradicate homosexuality and its entanglements from my life, that life would get better for me. At least that is the message I thought I was hearing.

I learned tools for overcoming what was referred to as life dominating sin and started to put them into practice. Things like, praying more, reading my bible more, and learning a life of self sacrifice. I heard that if I could deny my flesh more, I'd become more like Jesus. Lessons of becoming righteous in Him through changes in my behavior, and living obediently, also promised a positive outcome.

I came to believe that the life dominating sin in my life was homosexuality, I figured that all of these tools could be applied to find overcoming power. I was wrong. If I could overcome being gay, then certainly my life would be much better. I also heard that if I confessed my faults to others, then I would be forgiven from them. If I held them inside, I may not find the forgiveness and therefore not find the healing I was searching for.

My goal was to be the best Christian I could be. I took it that if I didn't get over homosexuality then my goals would be stifled and I would never find the overcoming power I so hungered to find.

In my search for answers to overcome homosexuality, I found special ministries that were designed just for someone like myself. They were called ex-gay ministries. Well, if I was to become the best at being a Christian, then it may mean that I needed to immerse myself into them. So, through my search, I discovered one that was looking for a staff person. I thought it might behoove me to take advantage of all that was available. I mean, after all, I had been praying for full time ministry and this must be custom designed for me!

I took a buyout from my job, which funded me with $30,000. I sold everything I couldn't take with me. I left close relationships including my two young daughters, packed up my car and moved across the country to find my pot of gold at the end of the rainbow! I was now going to rid myself of this gay thing, and find a life worthy of the calling of Christ as I was told I should live. The $30,000 was my financial ticket to freedom and I volunteered for the ministry for two years on my own dollar.

I did it all! Became the very best ex-gay I could become! I climbed all the way to the top. I was the director, the board member, the speaker, the teacher, and leader of the world's most well known specialized ministry that promised help to rid people of homosexuality.

I also sought marriage! To a woman! This also seemed to be the highest achievement one could accomplish as an official ex-gay. If I was all of these things, and married too, I must find that life I was searching for, a life worthy of the calling. I would have accomplished the required goal of ridding my life of homosexuality.

I learned how to share my story in the way that best told others of what had occurred in me. I had the miracle story of being free from homosexuality. I counted the years of freedom just like Alcoholics Anonymous does. No chips for me, but I could count, "One," "Five," "Ten," and I finally made it to "Twenty" years. I got all emotional every year around Valentine's Day because it was that week in 1984 that I had my last gay relationship. I didn't know how else to count the victory other than count from my last sexual act with a man and this marked the beginning of my freedom.

I tried to apply the lessons and thought that if I stuffed, and stuffed, and stuffed attractions, feelings, and anything within me that felt gay, I was doing what was right. Remaining clear of anything homosexual including any conversation that might glorify gay behaviors or mindsets promised that I might find deeper victory from the lure of any return to homosexuality.

I struggled with emotional attractions many years after my last homosexual sex encounter. I was taught that this was called Emotional Dependency and was also an idol to overcome. So, like other things I had learned, I became the expert in teaching on the destruction of emotional dependence upon another person. After learning how to protect myself from any emotional entanglements like that I had a new victory to talk about! I was now not only free from homosexual sex, but I was also free from emotional dependency!

Year by year, I gained pride, and self satisfaction that I had done what many had not, as seemed to be rare, I was experiencing the freedom from homosexuality, and emotional dependency that was sought after by so many. As someone who had a very public image, I had the amazing story and I had now made it over the twenty year mark! Wow! I was heading towards my Silver Anniversary of achievement.

However, what was going on inside me was a cauldron of pain, confusion, and fear. I was so high up on the leadership ladder within my circles, I didn't know who I could talk to? Who could I now confess my faults to? Internally, I knew that I hadn't achieved the goals of being a good Christian. I hadn't found freedom from my homosexuality. I was still as attracted to the hunky men as I always was! Everywhere I went, I found men that drew my eyes. It wasn't just because they were handsome, but it touched a very deep part of my sexual soul and I knew the difference. I had also successfully shut down my emotional needs in order to maintain my victory over any desires for another man's heart. I tried very hard to dismiss the momentary desires as temptation. I grieved, and grieved, thinking I would never again, ever, be close to a man like I had been before. I pushed it aside and just put one foot in front of the other trying to ignore my attractions, and desires.

Where could I go to talk about something that I believed was so strongly forbidden for discussion? We taught, and tried to practice not glorifying anything gay, so to talk about my inner desires, and hunger was not allowed as it seemed to glorify something from my past.

Therefore, as a leader, I certainly couldn't open up that conversation. "Oh, by the way, I am marking my twentieth year of sobriety from homosexuality," while I just held my breath as a great looking guy just walked by. I hadn't changed one wit! Not one wit!

Recently I discovered that underneath my lack of victory over my homosexual desires laid that Big Black Box of Shame. I didn't know I had been carrying this around from room to room, day by day, year by year. It was just a part of my life and I redefined it as being God's conviction or His discipline and redefined it as protection over my soul. It was painful, scary, and overwhelming much of the time.

I cursed it and yelled at it in my heart, since I couldn't talk about it. I was angry so many times when I perceived that it was blocking me from the victory I desired and I hadn't become the best ex-gay I could become since it was still there. I discovered a tremendous practice of stuffing all of the feelings that lay inside my soul.

I learned another thing that I thought I could strive for that would help. If I tried as hard as I could and faced all of the paralyzing fears of the world of straight men maybe I could become as though I were one of them! Yes, maybe this would help me find true freedom from homosexuality. So this also was woven into the ongoing plan. The world of ex-gays taught us that hanging around men could familiarize us with our own hidden masculinity.

So, I did that for years with great anxiety most of the time. I tried really hard but always felt distant, and a great challenge to fully relate to many discussions. But like all of the other tools we were given, I used this one with great hope that someday the anxiety would go away.

I never knew where to go for help with all of these inner conflicts. I mean, where would John Smid go to release all of this pent up stuff that had been building for over two decades? I knew all of the counselors in town for the most part. And I figured that certainly a Christian counselor would never want to hear all of this. I thought surely I would be told to continue with the tools I had been given and ongoing stuffing would be the result.

I've recently found out that I did have some choices. I could choose to no longer listen to the shame that came from the religious system. I realized that I had not chosen to be gay. I had nothing to do with the deep inner feelings, and needs that have loomed inside me for virtually my entire life. I had nothing to be ashamed about. So I dumped shame.

As I began to learn to live outside the shame I realized how much I had been wounded by a religious system that seemingly had taught me to live in denial and suppression regarding my homosexuality. The wounds created a great need to find some kind of comfort but since I was such a good boy, I didn't search the world for chemical comforts, and I certainly couldn't act out my secret sexual desires since that would surely cost me any hope of peace.

So, I got on the treadmill of ministry leadership and received many accolades for my service, and my testimony of freedom from homosexuality. Yes, this became my drug of choice. I was the hero child of the family and gained many invisible trophies for my accomplishments.

Through my recent honesty, I found a counselor that seemed to be a safe place to begin to unload years of stuffing. Upon my second meeting he made a profound observation. He told me that I talked through my feelings, rather than experiencing the feelings that were there. What? I was the guru of feeling oriented teaching for hundreds of people! How could he possibly be correct. I know my feelings well! I have been called emotionally intelligent by a good friend.

But, inside, I knew he was right. I was afraid to feel my feelings. If I truly began to open up, all of those years of stuffing would be released and I would surely die from the explosion. He went on to ask me if I were willing to work on this. Since I went to him for help, I believed I had to move forward with his observation and do some feeling work.

Wow!!! I had no idea all of that was underneath! I attended a group healing session under his guidance and found more anger and rage than I thought I could possibly hold. It was attached to the religious system that I believed had short changed me through the teaching of the tools of denial to help me find freedom. One of the first statements that came out of my mouth in a rage filled role play in a small group session was "YOU LIED TO ME!"

The very leaders of this system had not found the freedom for themselves that they promised I could have. As I looked back over the years I was given a duplicitous system. I knew some of them very personally, I knew they were living in the same denial that they taught me to live in and called itself sacrifice. I also released strong rage filled emotions about all of the enabling others who were living falsely. I acknowledged that many of these men I had known were still as gay as they ever were and yet they said they had found freedom.

In the recent years, I have reconnected with several people that I used to serve next to in our organizational ex-gay conferences and small groups. Not surprisingly, these guys have told me the same things I am saying here. We have found deep re-connections in our common life experiences. A discovery of not being alone in all of this is extremely comforting. I have found deeper friendships than I have had in many years. These relationships are often pointing me towards God, only this time with honestly at the foundation. They are encouraging me with a deeper understanding of God's true character of love and mercy than I have ever had before. They are also allowing me to grow in my own self discovery. I have people who are comforting me in my very personal grief, anger, and yes, they allow me to be enraged too. I have not felt any judgment, or criticism for my struggles in going through all this pain filled transition and have seen great patience from them as I waffle through this crooked path out of denial.

I discovered that I can own my own truth. I realize that it may not be THE truth, but it is my truth. My truth involves my life experience, my feelings, my thoughts and opinions. No one else has any place to attempt to deny that in my life. My truth evolves, changes, and can be challenged, but that is why it is my truth and not THE truth. I acknowledge that there is A TRUTH, that I continue to discover. But along the way I have permission to own my truth.

Today as a result of these profound revelations in my life, I have found a more solid ground to stand on. I feel more confident in myself, and more at peace with life as it is, not necessarily as I would have it. I find myself saying more and more, "it is, what it is."

I also learned a new version of the Serenity Prayer that began this whole process in my life way back in 1982.

> God, grant me the serenity to accept the people I cannot change – the courage to change the one I can – and the wisdom to know that it is me.

I fully realize that the things that have caused me such harm, and discouragement were not people but rather it has been a system that has blinded them just as it blinded me for so many years. I am learning that God never consigned us to secrecy and denial. He didn't ask me to hide my inner person and to live in shame. He never set up a plan to cause me to have to stuff such significant things in order to be a better servant of Him.

God designed a salvation plan that promised to set me free from shame. He provided a way for me to release the inner turmoil in complete honesty and asked me to declare this plan to others who are bound.

He said that I can confess my faults, all of them, to others, that I would be forgiven . He also said that THE truth, and my truth, and the truth that I will discover in the future, will set me free.

I'm getting more comfortable thinking about my heart's desire. I think I am finding it a little at a time because it is so threatening to me to think about. It's connected to love and relationship for sure. The nice big house is sold. Many of the office files are being shredded. Books given away to those who can use them. Personal belongings are being thinned out. I am preparing for the next place in life. I know that in order for my heart's desire to be fulfilled, I have to lessen the load and become a little more mobile.

God! Surprise Me! Is becoming a way of life. The old song *One Day at a Time, Sweet Jesus* is becoming a mantra that I repeat many times each day. As this book goes online, there are so many epilogues I can think of that could be written, but none are in place yet. That's tomorrow's surprise.

Epilogue

Walking Into the Lion's Den

As I compiled these chapters I felt it would be very important to have some words from Morgan Fox. He was very gracious and wrote his thoughts down to share.

By Morgan Jon Fox

In June 2005, when I joined many passionate people on the curb outside Love In Action in Memphis, Tennessee, our purpose was clear. We wanted to show that we cared deeply for anyone who was inside those walls against their will. We also had a great hope that we could put an end to what we clearly saw as an injustice. It was this strong and unified conviction that led us to put our daily lives aside and stand on the sidewalks of Love In Action. Our message was that being gay is OK, that God made us to live happy whole lives like anyone else, and that the world already mistreated and shunned many gay people enough.

We wanted to offer a voice of love and acceptance in the most immediate way we knew how in that very moment. We were a group of many people who came from different backgrounds, but one thing that linked us protestors was that we all felt it necessary to stand up for what we believed in, regardless of what would surely be a huge conflict ahead.

I learned a lot during that time during the summer of 2005, but the real learning for me came shortly after that. Admittedly, going into that summer I was someone who found it all too easy to jump to black-and-white conclusions about people on the opposite sides of issues I felt strongly about. But in an unlikely turn of events, the day I first met with John Smid in his office would hit me like a freight train.

All summer long John was the target of our lengthy campaign. He was the subject of many hours of research and planning in terms of our strategy to take on the opposition. And now here I was, walking into the lion's den to have a meeting with the lion himself.

I was nervous and uncertain how I would conduct myself; I was certainly unsure how he would respond. Part of me definitely envisioned a heated and potentially angry debate. I had written about five pages of potential issues and topics to address, and possible responses to what I figured would be his angry rebuttals. After all, many of us had spent an entire summer dedicating our lives to a task which created a huge obstacle and obfuscation of his daily life. So I was sure he wouldn't treat me kindly.

When I sat down in John's office, there was a brief moment of silence. I got really nervous, but then I took a deep breath, and something happened. I realized that if I came in arguing no one would win, and nothing would change. We would still both prove our individual points and leave with the same opinion of one another. I did not want to leave with that feeling.

What I wanted was to leave with a greater understanding of who this person was and where his organization was coming from. All of these thoughts quickly but quite clearly went through my mind in this brief silence, and so I took that deep breath and down came my walls. I said to John something like this: "It's kind of strange, because there's a lot of information about you on the internet, and I practically know your whole life story as a result, but you probably know nothing more about me than what has unfolded this summer as a result of an intense conflict." And I proceeded to spend about fifteen minutes telling him an abbreviated version of my life story. I'm so happy my decision in that brief moment of nervousness was to let go of my agenda and instead just try to make a connection, sharing my heart on a basic human level.

I got involved in the protest out of concern and love for people I truly felt were being harmed, and I wanted to show them there was another way. The interesting thing I learned that very day I first met with John Smid was that the reason he was involved with Love In Action was out of concern and love for people he truly felt were being harmed, and he wanted to show them another way.

How interesting this was to look across a desk at my enemy and realize he truly believed and felt wholeheartedly he was acting out of love and passion, just as I thought and knew that I was! John also notably didn't take an angry or aggressive stance that I was sure he'd take towards me. That was a powerful moment for me, and that began a process for me of learning how to relate to and communicate with people who had dynamically opposing views from my own. I still strongly disagreed with this man, but I could no longer deny that he was human, and acting out of what he perceived as love, just as I was.

Over time, as John and I began to meet more often, we had long conversations about what was going on in our lives. We both shared deeply personal things about our families and friends. We didn't debate, or argue about our differences. This allowed a chance for two people to find out they had plenty in common without dwelling on what made them opposites. It created a mutual respect that would lay the foundation for growth and trust. It opened the door for something I never could have seen coming—a friendship. This is something that eventually became somewhat of a conflict for me.

A few friends of mine questioned why I was befriending someone that still represented so many things they viewed as hurtful and harmful towards gay people. Along this road John had left his post at Love In Action and I began to see more and more change in him, and accordingly, I would try to explain that I saw John opening up and beginning to see things in a different light. Not that he was the only one doing the changing here, as it was apparent I too was becoming more open and willing to dialogue and communicate in a way that allowed him not to feel threatened by me.

Many would ask me, "How can you sit there and not lash out at him?" I'm sure many people thought I was being weak, that I was letting John manipulate me into thinking he was something he was not. I viewed this all quite differently. I saw it as an incredible opportunity to learn the valuable tools of mature and fair communication, building the foundation for a relationship that our society doesn't readily nurture. But the real test of our unlikely friendship was one that was about to occur, and I had to ask the hard questions ..... Was I being naïve, was this appropriate, Was I being naïve? Was it healthy? and Where would it eventually lead?

In March 2010 John wrote an apology letter. As I had heard reflected in many conversations that we were having, he addressed that he had experienced change in his heart, and was sorry if during his time at Love In Action, in their teenage program Refuge, and with Exodus International, he had harmed anyone. He also encouraged people to write him and give him a chance to directly address this, as he felt he could communicate in a much different way now that his heart had changed.

While many people felt this apology was a breakthrough, and applauded it, there were those who didn't trust it. Some felt it wasn't enough, or that it wasn't done correctly. I even got involved in this a bit, as I stood up for John and encouraged people to give him a chance to get to know him as I did. In a meeting during this time period I also challenged John, asking deeper questions, echoing many of the concerns I saw in reaction to his apology letter. These potentially difficult conversations were surprisingly easy, because John and I had gained a trust for one another over time. The only problem came down to the fact that for the first time, I had to tread through the reality that this private friendship was symbolic of something much greater on a very public level.

Over the years since the protests, I had become friends with many people who had attended Love In Action, as they shared their stories with me for the documentary I was making. These individuals had a much different beginning to their relationship with John, and therefore would have to take a much different path towards finding peace within it.

Part of learning how to form a relationship with someone I had once considered an enemy was realizing the complexities of the very nature of relationships. I absolutely have to honor those people who've had different life experiences with John than I have. It's important for me to continually acknowledge that although I may feel safe and comfortable being friends with someone at supposedly the opposite end of the spectrum, others may not, and I must be sensitive to this and how it may affect them. Each individual on either side must make their own journey, and it's important for me to remain honest and aware along this path.

This is a constant test, but perhaps one of the most important to me. How do we build relationships with people we see as our enemy? How do we maintain these relationships without compromising what we believe or purely promoting our own agenda? How do we decide it's OK to give someone another chance if we have shared a part of our lives with this person and as a result experienced hurt or harm? I do not think it's always safe to give people second chances. I believe that sometimes it's important for people to heal without necessarily letting people in their lives that may represent the pain they've felt. For me what I have learned is that I can personally make the strides I need to make in my life, and work as hard as I can towards balancing being a fair, honest, and forgiving person, who listens and is willing to learn.

I am incredibly grateful that John and I formed a friendship, as I have and continue to learn so much from it, and from him. However, it is impossible to acknowledge and honor this friendship without recognizing the conflicts that are very real and also symbolic of a greater spectrum of issues that are often quite divisive in our world today. In the end, the central lesson I take away from this is that just because I feel safe, doesn't mean others do, and it's very important for me to honor and respect those who do not. We all deserve to feel safe. We all deserve to feel cared for and loved. And we all deserve to have advocates in the moments we are most vulnerable and unable to lift our own voices. It is my hope that we may work toward a goal of raising these voices of concern, to continually broaden our understanding to a point that perhaps we may all find it easier to approach and communicate with one another . . . to hear each other's hearts, to find it within ourselves to forgive those who've hurt us, and make the necessary strides to mend the wounds of those we've harmed.

I often wonder what might have happened if I had just walked into John's office that fateful day in June 2005 and had a conversation with him, as opposed to standing on the street participating in a protest. Would things have happened differently? Was there a better approach? While I do not doubt a different approach could have been taken instead of protesting with megaphones and engaging in some heated curbside conflicts with Love In Action's staff at times, I also do not regret it for a second.

In fact, I believe that the very reason I was able to sit in the lion's den and not be afraid, letting my guard down, was because we had both engaged in a conflict that allowed us both the time and space to do some real thinking.

My conclusion is that conflict isn't necessarily always bad. Sometimes conflict may even be necessary, and healthy—if it is a process that opens us up and allows us to learn from it, and if it is nonviolent and motivated by love. Perhaps healthy conflict can lead us to a place where we stand our ground and boldly represent what we believe, and as a result feel more affirmed and comfortable at the very moment when we decide it's safe to let our guard down.

About the Author

John was raised in Omaha, Nebraska. He grew up with two older sisters and a younger half sister and brother. He was raised in a middle class neighborhood, attended high school and shortly after he graduated he began a 13 year stint working for the Union Pacific Railroad.

He got married the first time at just 19 years old to a high school girlfriend. They had two daughters. John discovered his homosexuality late in life and encountered his first sexual activity with a man after six years of marriage. John decided to divorce his wife and move towards an open gay life. During a four year period he had several significant relationships one of which lasted for three years.

After a couple of years and a series of disappointments he began to experience some internal conflict which led him to find a deeper faith in God in 1982. This led him into another conflict. How would his faith correlate with his homosexual relationships?

In 1984 he decided to break away from all associations with his gay friends and community. He found some friends within a local church and singles ministry. He developed a deep connection with the singles pastor who embraced John and his story with grace. John began to be involved within the leadership of this ministry. He also developed a pantomime clown ministry called Clowns Created by Christ with 12 other fellow single Christians.

While fulfilling friendships, and his volunteer work with the singles ministry were satisfying, John still wanted to learn more about his past life of living within the gay community. John found an ex-gay ministry and made the decision to move from Omaha to San Rafael to work with Love In Action in 1986.

He met his wife, Vileen, while in the singles ministry. They dated some before John's move and continued to build on their relationship long distance. After two years they married in 1988.

John's work with ex-gay ministry continued for 22 years through 2008. Gaining a well known status within national leadership with the covering ministry, Exodus International, John invested almost his entire adult life within these ministry organizations.

Addressing complex and controversial issues with finesse and candor, John uses the mirror of his own life experiences to reflect the challenges that confront us all, as well as the common answers we each seek.

Whether he is dealing one-on-one with an individual, a family, or speaking in churches or seminars nationwide, John's message of openness and honesty resonates with everyone who longs to be accepted, loved, and understood.

His story has been told in periodicals such as the *San Francisco Chronicle, New York Times, Washington Post, San Diego Union Tribune,* and the *Wall Street Journal.* John's rare blend of insights and inspiration has been featured on numerous broadcasts such as *Larry King Live, CNN, CNN Medical News, Good Morning America,* and *ABC's 20/20*

Today, he is the Executive Director of the nondenominational Grace Rivers Ministry, based in Memphis, Tennessee. After much soul-searching and changes in his approach to life challenges, John is helping others to look at their life honestly, to receive God's love fully, and to love others regardless of their color, opinions, faiths, or life experiences.

Relationships are important to John. This theme has played a commanding role both in his history and ministry. And the best example of it can be found in the fatherly pride he shows in his two daughters, four grandchildren, and over two-decade marriage to Vileen, who served as a quiet strength behind the Smid family's ongoing quest to seek Christ.

A New Life

A life reflection by John J. Smid

Psalm 116:1-2

I love the LORD, for he heard my voice, He heard my cry
for mercy. Because he turned his ear to me, I will call on
him as long as I live.

"John, you need to know Jesus! We are Christians and we want you
to know that you need Him. I know all that you have been involved in
and that doesn't matter, all that matters is that you accept Jesus into
your life."

My head spun around several times while listening to these two girls.
I had known them for a long time. We graduated from high school
together. It was two o'clock in the morning and I had stopped by the
local pancake house with my friends after our night at the bar but I
wasn't ready for what I heard that night.

This was a different experience for me. I had never heard anyone
speak about Jesus that way much less from these two girls. What had
happened in their life to bring about such a dramatic shift? Well, I didn't

really take the time to find out—I just wanted out of there. I went to a table where my friends were and they had all gone. I felt abandoned and insignificant since they didn't tell me they were leaving or even to say goodbye! Maybe they heard some of the conversation and were scared too!

This was the first time for me to experience what many call evangelical Christianity but it wouldn't be the last. I guess this was the hammer and chisel that would start the crack in my hardened life to spread. A short time later I changed offices at my job and found myself sitting right behind another lady. She was quite friendly and very energetic about life. It was apparent that she was connected to most of the other people working near us as she laughed with them, talked with them and yes, she was also very excited about something else – Jesus!

Pat took a different approach than I had experienced in the pancake house. She was friendly and interested in other people's lives. She quickly found out that I was recently divorced from my first wife and was living a pretty active party life. I talked about going to the bars, being out with friends and that I was pretty happy with my new found freedom from my marriage. Oh, I told her about my two children and tried to seem excited about that too but in reality, I didn't know much about what was happening with my daughters because I had other priorities.

Pat had things all over her desk that were evidence of her priorities. She talked about her own divorce, her past life of alcohol and partying around. She talked of her upbringing in a Catholic family. I related to that quickly as I too had grown up Catholic. We now had common ground. Her experience with the bars and such as well as our religious background became common conversation.

Now, about those things on her desk; magnets, books, pamphlets, and a worn Bible were all very present. A worn Bible? What is that? I thought you needed to protect them because they were special. Pat told me otherwise. I remember her telling me how she wrote in it and used it every day. That seemed so foreign to me that I kept asking her about this Bible she seemed to feel so special about. She gave me answers as she could.

But I mostly remember that Pat didn't seem to be all that interested in my weekend life. She also didn't seem shocked by it—seemingly since she had been there herself.

After a few months and our relationship became more comfortable, she said she wanted me to meet a friend of hers. His name was Jerry. I don't remember where or how we met but it seemed that Jerry was a lot like Pat. He too was friendly and was up front about having been through a lot of stuff in his life like I did. Like Pat, he seemed to be real, and easy to talk with.

"John, there is a group at my church that I'd like you to meet. They are a singles group and this weekend they are having a social time. There will be food and these people aren't scary. Why don't you come?"

I was curious by this time. I was also not doing so well myself. I had experienced many painful disappointments in my relationships that I wasn't really sharing with Pat, or her friend Jerry. I didn't want to admit that my life wasn't going so hot. But, in reality, I was looking for something different.

I didn't go to the group that she was talking about but it remained in my memory as an option if things got worse, which they eventually did. Instead, my first attempt to get help came through an invitation to an al-anon group. My friends said there were better people there than I had been hanging around. Well, my lust and pain came together and I was motivated to attend this group.

"Hello, my name is Cindy, John. I can relate to what you just said. I have been there myself and I understand. I found help in praying the Serenity Prayer."

What? REAL help in praying? Well, I needed real help. Cindy's expression of common ground once again motivated me. She understood! Maybe I should try her prayer! The next Sunday I was going through the lowest of lows and feeling suicidal. I got out the prayer she mentioned and began to repeat its words. Something grabbed me that day; something very different. I felt relieved of some of the pain I was feeling. Could it have been the prayer? Could God have been listening to me? Is He real?

One particular night on which I was struggling, Pat called to talk with me about something. She heard my struggle and said, "Jerry and I are coming over". They came to my house and talked with me for a while and offered to pray with me. I remember how accepted and loved I felt that this lady and her friend cared enough to go out of their way to show me their concern and their support.

I started to ponder the events I had experienced concerning God, Jesus, religion and my life. Maybe there is something to this Jesus thing that I heard at the pancake house. These people that I had met seemed energized about their experiences with Jesus. They also have had trouble in their lives and they didn't seem as afraid to talk about it as I was.

"Pat, maybe I'll go to one of those social events you spoke about. Is there anyone there like us?" She gave me directions and I went to someone's house and there were lots of people there eating, laughing, and talking. I felt really strange there largely because I didn't know anyone. But, Pat was right, they were having fun and it was apparent that their life was different than mine and yet, the same.

I went back to my life and friends and tried to make it again. I was determined that I was going to succeed with my plans. After all, I didn't give up a family, marriage, and my children for nothing. I was invested in my decision – and being right! For a while it went better but not for long. I found more pain, more discouragement, and my pride wouldn't let me go further in talking about it openly.

Pat had often invited me to her church. She explained that it was different than maybe the ones I had experienced. There was hand clapping, lively music, and it wasn't like our common Catholic background. She also said that I wouldn't have to go alone and that she would meet me there and maybe Jerry would be there as well. Well I was up for something new and interesting so I finally decided to go. The day before I had bought some new shoes and clothes for a special date with a new friend I had gone on. I got these new clothes out to wear to church. Hum, that sounded weird, church. I am going to church!

I sat on the aisle and before the service, the pastor, John Walker, was walking down the aisle and stopped at my seat. "Hello, I am Pastor John Walker, you have a beautiful yellow sweater on. What is your name?" Oh, if he'd only known what happened in that sweater the night before. But, I enjoyed the compliment and that he took the time to introduce himself.

I wasn't ready for any more church for a while. I had to process what I had experienced. I enjoyed it; well as much as I could, considering how strange it was for me. At the same time in my life there was another person who was excited about Jesus. She was the sister to Joe, a man that I had a three year relationship with. Her name was Jeannie.

Joe told me Jeannie was a Jesus Freak and that she lived differently than we did. After all, I was in a sexual relationship with her brother, Joe, and Jeannie knew that was the case. She didn't seem to make that a big deal. We would eat at her house and enjoy her funny sense of humor and friendliness.

One week, Jeannie called me to invite me to her church. She said they were having a revival. What? What in the world is a revival? Well, here we go again, something strange to experience. I guess I'll go. I didn't die from the last church experience I had. Maybe this will be equally interesting.

I surely wasn't prepared for what would transpire this night. I went in, sat down with her and entered into one of the most life changing events I had ever had. I do not know what was said from the front or who I was sitting next to but I clearly heard something in my head. "John, you don't have to live this way any longer." What? Who said that? Well, it wasn't quite that shocking, but it was life changing, no doubt.

The voice continued on, "John, go and ask Laurie to go to dinner with you." Laurie was a friend from a community theater I as a part of. I didn't know her very well but she was a nice girl and really friendly. So, that night I went home and called Laurie. She said yes! So, Friday we're on for dinner.

In our discussion Laurie was as friendly as I had hoped. She was also honest about her life. Well, you guessed it, Laurie was also a Christian. There were other things we had in common. Laurie was also divorced. But there was something even more important that came out that evening. Laurie's first husband was gay. I had made quite a deep investment in a decision to leave my family and live out my life as a gay man with other gay men. I was searching for common ground, understanding, and for sure I wanted to feel heard by someone who knew what it was like to have a life like mine.

This was quite the shocking experience. God must have known. Did Jesus really see my life from the inside out? Even more significant, did Jesus hear the cry of my heart? I can't make sense of all of these people who I met with excitement about this Jesus, but is it true? Can something about my life significantly change? The voice said that I had a choice. That voice said I could live life differently and that the deep pain I had been experiencing could go away.

My friends Pat, Jerry, Jeannie, Laurie, all had something in common. They seemed to have a relationship with Jesus and weren't afraid to talk about it. But they had something else in common. They freely talked about their life stories. They told me about the mistakes, the pain, the choices, and the freedom they had all experienced. They were all real people with real life issues and seemingly had found a real Jesus that understood and accepted them.

After meeting with Laurie I had experienced enough of this Jesus that I began to look into this phenomenon. Pat gave me a $3 paperback Bible. I began to read it. It was really quite interesting, since I was reading it for the first time like a book, rather than chapter and verse references. I began to understand my life was broken from the beginning and I was in need of someone greater than myself who could rescue me. I found out that the gospel was not a religion, but it was a gift to John Smid from a living Savior to offer me eternity with Him.

My life did in fact begin to change. My priorities were different now. The change was slow and clumsy. Joe and I had separated and I thought it might be better to find another man that would love me and was not so thrown off by my new found zeal. That wasn't hard. I met a man named Paul that fit the bill. On our first time together alone he told me he loved me and that he was a Christian. He taught at a Christian school, no less. He was a great guy. But I wasn't so great. Our relationship became as tumultuous as all of the others because I was so conflicted and torn I didn't know how to maintain a relationship very well. Almost immediately I returned to my relationship with Joe.

The pain continued as if my life were on a pendulum swing. Up, down, up, down, up, down—and I was becoming even more troubled. What should I do now? I had been praying a simple prayer daily. "God, get me out of this." On February 10, 1984 I made the decision to call, Joe, and tell him I was leaving the relationship. We had broken up a couple of times before but this time something was different. We hadn't been doing so well and it just seemed necessary to make the break.

The next week I attended the weekly gathering of those single folks that I had met the year before. I thought maybe they could help me and replace the friends that I was leaving behind. They did. They came through with flying colors. I continued on with their weekly group and I even went to that church every Sunday. It didn't seem so strange to me anymore. I grew in understanding of their faith, their relationship with each other, and their Jesus. I had become like those girls four years earlier. I was now excited about what I had found in Jesus.

That was a long time ago. A lot has changed in my life for sure but it began with a few people who were willing to share their life with me. These folks had something in common that has stuck with me through the years. They were vulnerable, honest from their hearts, and weren't afraid to tell me about their lives—including their mistakes and short-comings. I wasn't a project to be completed; rather I felt like a person they desired to know. Someone they cared about but weren't trying to control or condemn.

It isn't so strange that I would feel the burden to continue in a life that reaches those that are hurting or lost. The people who reached out to me practiced loving acceptance without judgment. They weren't using a systematic approach to reaching me. They were just being them-selves. With God's help, they didn't hide underneath a false religion. They didn't separate themselves from me as though they had arrived to some higher plane of living.

Each of them knew their shortcomings and they lived in the grace of a loving God. They just wanted me to know the Jesus they had met because He had loved them while they were yet sinners.

After a few years of being single I was married to Vileen in 1988. My two daughters have grown into mothers and I have four grandchildren. As I look at my grandkids, I recognize each day that the gifts that were shared with me those many years ago have now transcended into a second generation of life! I certainly wouldn't be where I am today if it weren't for those loving people who cared enough about me to share their Jesus with me. I do not believe I would have survived this life if it weren't for Christ saving my life and changing my path.

I am not sure I really know how to thank each person who has had an effect on my life through their own honesty. The numbers are far too great to share with each one of them. Some of them have gone on to other places and I am not sure I could even locate them. I do have friendships with some of them and I try to often tell them how much their lives have meant to me. I may have some that I haven't adequately thanked.

This is my new life that remains new every day. His mercies are new every morning for sure. I need Jesus today just like I did all the years before but didn't know it. The only difference is that I know Him now and can call upon Him freely. I also recognize His grace not so much for the sins I commit every day because I know those were forgiven before I even thought to commit them. I recognize His grace for my humanness! The fact that I was born into a sinful, broken world requires His sacrifice at the cross for my eternity.

In the end, my greatest thanksgiving goes to Jesus Christ for His salvation that came upon our brothers and sisters from the beginning that is passed down generation to generation. This is my story. Well, part of my story. There isn't enough paper to contain all of it. Each time I think back over my life, there are many more things to say about Jesus and me.

As you can imagine, Jesus drew me to Himself through letting me know that He heard me. He understood my plight and joined with me for life. He forgave me and continues to work with me to change my life one day at a time. This recent chapter in my journey certainly has been a surprise.

God is in the renewing and restoring business. I have experienced an amazing life do over several times. He has graciously allowed me to make amends, restore old broken relationships, and enjoy sweet renewals over and over.

John J. Smid - Speaker

The signature of John Smid's vocational ministry is his honest, vulnerable, straight forward and open style. He won't just teach ethereal information. No matter what John is speaking about, his life application and story are always included in what he has to share.

Throughout his speaking career, Smid has addressed some very complex and highly controversial issues with finesse and open candor. From his own vulnerability he helps everyone to know they are surely not alone in life's challenges. John's deep seated faith brings courage to stay the course and find the solutions that will bring personal victory.

Because he handles his life as an open book, you will easily to relate to his story and your heart will open up to receive the wisdom he has to impart. His speaking influence stems from many years of experience dealing with individuals and families seeking significant changes in their life.

Having facilitated or taught countless groups throughout the tenure of his full time Christian ministry, the insights he has to share stem from hundreds of real lives, real stories, and real victories. John has spoken in numerous venues and churches from many diverse backgrounds. He also has shared his story in nearly all of the fifty states and three continents. His message of openness and honesty is universal to the inner desire of most people to be known, heard, and understood.

John's reputation has been primarily associated with having served with and led the charge of Love In Action International for 22 years. He served on the board of directors for Exodus International for 11 years. He is certainly familiar with the inner workings of what has long been known as ex-gay ministry. Being gay himself, John's connection to these organizations stemmed from his own personal life experience and he is gifted as sharing his journey with honesty and integrity.

Go to the Grace Rivers Event's page for further information on requesting John to speak.

About Grace Rivers Ministry

Our Mission

Grace Rivers is a ministry with the gay community that reveals the message of an authentic relationship with Jesus Christ and genuine community with His followers – because every person deserves to know that Jesus loves them. (John 3:16-17)

> We are followers of Jesus Christ, Impacting our Community One Person at a Time.

It is our greatest desire to see Christ transform His people. We hope that He may use Grace Rivers as one instrument to do this. We have learned that honesty and authenticity are the vehicles to see the fruit of the Spirit flourish in our lives. We invite you to look through the pages of the Grace Rivers website to see events, articles and tools to reflect our desire. It is our hope you will see Jesus reflected in the truths set forth here.

Our Story

The beginnings of Grace Rivers ministry can be traced back to 2007 when a new burden began to grow inside John. He desired to reach out to the entire body of Christ, helping men and women to remove their masks of fear. It was his thought that their fear could block their effectiveness in the kingdom of God.

In November of 2007, John shared this burden with his pastor, Dana Key. After much prayer and time spent in counsel, he was convinced that God was calling him to leave the ministry of Love in Action and move forward into a renewed vision for God's kingdom.

By faith, John resigned from Love In Action in May 2008, still growing in the understanding of God's call. His church appointed him to lead a small group study introducing his teachings which he titled Tributaries of Grace. This series of teachings was the foundation for what has become the ministry's signature message, The Journey of Grace.

The series was well received. As families came forward with relationship struggles, John put together a conference just for them. This became the model for what is now the Families of Grace conference.

In September of 2008, a steering committee was formed to test the feasibility of forming a non-profit entity bearing the name Grace Rivers Ministry. After several meetings and much prayer, the committee formed the vision, the mission, and the core values of Grace Rivers. They made the official recommendation for Smid to form the ministry, with some of the Steering Committee going on to form the first Board of Directors. Celebrated at his home church with friends, church members, and ministry supporters, Grace Rivers had its official launch party on December 2nd, 2008.

Today, because of John Smid's vast experience with men and women facing homosexuality in their lives, Grace Rivers has narrowed its vision to be a ministry with the gay community that reveals the message of an authentic relationship with Jesus Christ and genuine community with His followers – because every person deserves to know that Jesus loves them.

www.gracerivers.com

Resources

Evangelicals Concerned
http://www.ecinc.org

The Gay Christian Network
http://www.gaychristian.net/

The Evangelical Network
http://www.t-e-n.org/

Courage Trust - United Kingdom
http://www.courage.org.uk/

Recommended Reading

The Velvet Rage: Overcoming the Pain of Growing Up Gay in a Straight Man's World, by Alan Downs, Ph.D.
Homosexianity, by Pastor R. D. Weekly
The Children Are Free, by Rev. Jeff Miner an John Tyler Connoley
Exchanging the Truth of God for a Lie, by Jeremy Marks
Love is an Orientation, by Andrew Marin
And You Invited Me In, by Cheryl Moss Tyler
Gay Conversations With God, by James Alexander Langteaux

Videos

For the Bible tells Me So, by Daniel Karslake
This is What Love In Action Looks Like, by Morgan Jon Fox

Made in the USA
Charleston, SC
22 March 2013